Cookie Cooks

KITCHEN PRESS

First published in Scotland by Kitchen Press, 1 Windsor Place, Dundee, DD2 1BG

Text copyright Melanie McCallum & Domenico Del Priore

Illustrations copyright Conzo Throb www.conzo.co.uk

Designed & typeset by Anti Limited www.anti-limited.com

A CIP catalogue record for this book is available from the British Library.

ISBN: 978-0-9570373-2-8

Printed and bound in Scotland by Bell & Bain Ltd.

To all those who eat with us

Acknowledgements

Thanks to Emily for the idea, Frances for the recipes and Amelia for inspiration.

Contents

Introduction

Cookie is our restaurant in Glasgow which has an open kitchen at its heart. We are Scottish and Italian, with a family here in Scotland and another home with a large, productive olive grove in Umbria, Italy. Food and all that it means is our shared interest. Our two professional backgrounds collided when we opened Cookie in the southside of the city, delivering quality food, educating and engaging people with what they eat.

We are essentially all about getting people interested in food, sharing knowledge and recipes, traditions and culture. We run a barter system with local allotment gardeners, and often they will grow specific items for our chefs. We use local producers and source all of our products individually. We can tell you the story behind everything available in Cookie. Our menu changes regularly, depending on what's in season, what's available or what interests us.

The aim of Cookie is to keep cooking alive, and part and parcel of that is ensuring that food traditions are passed on from one generation to the next. This needs communication and human interaction. Since Cookie is about people, we've written the book around the core characters in our lives. The recipes are, therefore, not divided into starters, mains and puddings but into chapters based around our family members – all of whom have shared their favourite recipes – and the things they love to eat.

We hope you enjoy them.

Melanie and Domenico

Essentials

*There are a few essential items that are so key to how we eat
that they need a little introduction of their own: bread, olive oil,
wine, Pecorino and guanciale.*

Bread

There are two undeniable truths of baking your own bread. Firstly, once you do, you won't want to buy bread again and, secondly, it's so much easier than you would imagine. At Cookie we bake all our own bread.

When we were collating the recipes it was difficult to see just where to put bread. Grandma always baked bread when I was a child. All that was offered in rural Scotland in the 1970s was sliced, tasteless and white, so she baked her own every week. As a young woman living in more cosmopolitan places, I never baked – I was so much more liberated, so much more of a career woman. That is, until about twenty years ago when life took me to Bermuda... a beautiful tropical island lacking one thing: a good bakery. I phoned home and got some transatlantic instructions and an airmail package of dried yeast. It turned out to be easy and I've baked my own bread ever since.

So, why doesn't everyone bake bread? I think what puts people off might be the yeast. In the community classes we ran for kids, we gave a whole lesson on yeast and let them experiment. I'd recommend this to anyone. We told them the story of the 'invention' of bread: how the ancient Egyptians ground grains and mixed them with water to a thick paste, how one day someone left this out in the sun too long and it reacted with the naturally occurring yeasts in the air. The yeast

grew, ate some of the grains' starch, made air bubbles, and the paste puffed up. And tasted better. Our kids' classes produce fantastic bread. It really is that easy: if a six year old can bake it, anyone can. There are just a few rules…

General Rules of Bread Making

- Yeast has been commercially available since the 19th century. At Cookie our chef uses fresh yeast; at home I use dried, but never the fast-acting dried variety as I think it has a strange, artificial taste. As a rule of thumb, if you're using fresh yeast use double the quantity given for dried.

- You need a hot oven and a few hours for proving and kneading. It's worth remembering that bread is forgiving stuff and it's hard to go wrong. Many times I've left bread proving for hours as life gets in the way – just knock it back, give it a quick knead and wait for it to rise again.

- Wholemeal flour needs roughly $\frac{1}{3}$ again of the liquid in a recipe for white flour.

- A dough mixer makes life easy, as kneading by hand can be laborious. If you are using your hands, make the dough into a circle. Flour your work surface well and stretch the dough between your two hands, then fold it back on top of itself before turning the dough and stretching another side of the circle. It will start to feel smooth and more and more elastic under your hands as the yeast reacts. You should knead it twice – first for ten minutes or so, and then, once it's risen and you've punched the air out, for another five.

- You can't part-bake bread. Our chef tells me the part-baked breads available rely on a chemical to let the process stop half way through. With real bread, if you take the loaf out of the oven and it's not ready, you need to put it back in immediately. If you let it cool while it is still doughy, you will be stuck with doughy bread.

- The bread is cooked if it sounds hollow when you hold it and tap on the base.

- There are all sorts of specialist instructions out there on bread baking if you want to get expert at it. I would recommend starting on some simple loaves and then getting more adventurous.

Olive Oil

We pick olives and produce olive oil from our land in Italy every year. It is an annual gathering of family and friends in the first half of November in a small town called Amelia in Southern Umbria. Amelia has produced prized olive oil for over 2500 years. The oil is famous the world over for its perfect balance of flavours.

Olive picking creates a rural gathering: a time to meet neighbours, drink the local wine and talk about the year that has been. People bring their olives to the local cooperative press where they are washed and mashed and the oil extracted. Fresh virgin olive oil is the most prized. It is green, grassy and peppery – a fantastic taste very different to what you might expect. At this stage, it's used for drizzling on salads and bruschetta, or really anywhere that lets you enjoy the flavour.

Olive oil is an annual product. As it ages through the year and into the next it loses its intensity of flavour and becomes more suitable to cook with. Our oil gets to Cookie as soon as we can get it there, which is usually within days of the pressing. This is normally in the first week of November.

Each year our oil is slightly different, depending on the weather that year, which adds to the interest. It has vintage.

Wine

When we opened Cookie we became wine importers and producers. We did this to allow our customers to taste the beautiful simplicity of farm wine from our region in Italy. It was also a political choice to support small producers rather than big industry players who, by their nature, make the world homogeneous.

Lots of adjectives which I find hard to spell are often used to describe wine. For most of the people I come across in Glasgow, these descriptions are a big turn-off. I'm an Italian-Glaswegian and wine was always part of the meal. 'Vino da Tavola' or Table Wine just means wine to have with food. My wine knowledge was gained by drinking it and by hanging out with the people who make it. To put it simply, Cookie stocks a lot of the wine made by my mates or their friends.

The wines we stock at Cookie are the wines I really like to drink. If something takes my fancy, I go and find out about it, call the producer, and go and see where it's made. The people making the wine we sell are all small European producers; each one expresses the character of the person who made it and the place they come from. I really like that idea. It is also the reason why we almost exclusively sell European wines.

I'm driven by aesthetics, so I think about the land where the wine was made, and what the locals eat in that region. If you examine wine from this perspective, you find that the food from the area goes really well with the wine they drink — there are no pairing problems. Did they cut the grass around the vine or leave the wild flowers to grow beneath? Was there a rose bush at the end of the field, how much did they cut back, did they pick early or late? All these questions tell you something about the wine and hint at the character of the person who made it.

I'm really enjoying working with Alessandro from Sandonna, a small producer from the centre of Italy. We took his great farm wine, tweaked it to make it transportable, and it became Cookie A: a great Vino Rosso. Now we are working on Cookie B, our house white wine based around Grechetto grapes blended with Trebbiano. Next year we will try Chardonnay.

Each year produces something new. Finding and discovering great wine is a journey which always takes you somewhere different, like life itself. In general, beware of too much oak, a sugary softness and a blended consistency: they are the hallmarks of wine producers' trickery, of mutton dressed as lamb.

Pecorino

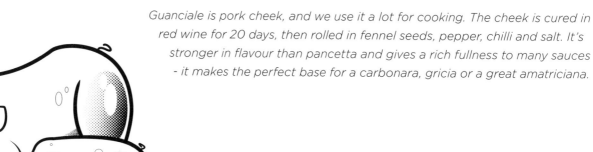

'Pecora' means 'sheep' in Italian. There are hundreds of different types of sheep's milk cheeses in Italy, sometimes mixed with cow's or goat's milk. So when you buy Pecorino, it is important to think about what it is for. We use Pecorino Romano for cooking. It is not as fatty as Parmesan: hard and salty, it is perfect for grating. It's an ancient cheese which was a staple of Roman legionnaires.

Guanciale

Guanciale is pork cheek, and we use it a lot for cooking. The cheek is cured in red wine for 20 days, then rolled in fennel seeds, pepper, chilli and salt. It's stronger in flavour than pancetta and gives a rich fullness to many sauces - it makes the perfect base for a carbonara, gricia or a great amatriciana.

Bruno
(Nonno)

Bruno is Domenico's dad, the Nonno of our family.

He was born in Salerno, the youngest of a large family. Salerno is on the beautiful Amalfitano coast, at the foot of Vesuvius – all fertile land and sunshine. Think sun-ripened tomatoes, citrus fruit, fresh fish, basil and greens which are unique to the lava-rich soil, full of iron and flavour.

Bruno was also, as he reminds us, a child of the war. His cooking is firmly grounded in economy, respect for good ingredients and the all-important activity of shopping correctly. This type of shopping, particularly for vegetables and fruit, is an art. Take your time, examine everything carefully, ask where it's from, discuss at length and ultimately haggle a bit on price.

Life took Bruno to Scotland in the 1960s where he struggled with the discovery that olive oil was only available in tiny quantities from pharmacists for purely medicinal use, and that aubergines were called "queer gear". He adapted, became lifelong friends with the local wholesalers, made frequent stock up drives to Italy, and continued cooking his mother's recipes. We have long wanted to record them, as many are the most popular dishes in Cookie.

Nowadays, the once exotic has become commonplace, but it is important to understand the real origins of these recipes and the traditional way of making them to ensure sure these traditions are carried forward.

Zucchini Flowers

Makes 20

vegetable oil for deep frying

150g '00' or plain flour

1 free range egg

100ml sparkling
mineral water

1 tbsp vegetable oil

20 very fresh
courgette flowers

250g mozzarella, chopped
into 20 small pieces

10 salted anchovies, rinsed
and chopped in half

sea salt

freshly ground black pepper

These are a summer treat in Italy and a standard southern Italian starter. They can be done with or without anchovies depending on your preference.

Fill your deep frying pan with vegetable oil and put on a medium heat.

To make the batter, sift the flour into a large bowl, then whisk in the egg and the mineral water, season and add a tablespoon of vegetable oil. Whisk until you have smooth batter.

Stuff the flowers by cutting them gently across the top and placing a piece of mozzarella and half an anchovy inside each. Check your oil is hot enough for deep frying (test it with a cube of bread which should start sizzling at once), then dip each flower in the batter and fry until golden and puffy. Drain on kitchen paper and serve immediately.

Rizi e Bisi

Serves 4

This is a fantastic winter and spring dish: easy to make with fresh or frozen peas, and quite different from a risotto. The rice to use for this is carnaroli rice which, like the dish, comes from Venice. At a push, arborio or even basmati will taste good.

Melt the butter with the olive oil in a wide-bottomed pan on a low heat. Add the onion and pancetta and cook gently for 5 minutes, until the onion is soft and the pancetta is starting to brown at the edges. Stir in the parsley and the peas, if you're using fresh ones (if you're using frozen peas, you'll add them later on).

Pour in two ladlefuls of stock and mix everything gently. Simmer for 5 minutes, then add the remaining stock and season to taste. Bring to the boil and stir in the rice. Simmer gently until the rice is *al dente*, turning it often with a spoon. If you're using frozen peas, add them once the rice has been simmering for about 10 minutes.

The finished dish should be like a thick soup. To finish, stir in a tablespoon of butter, plenty of fresh Parmesan and serve hot.

60g butter

4 tbsp olive oil

1 onion, finely chopped

50g pancetta, finely chopped

1 handful of flat-leaf parsley, finely chopped

1kg peas in their pods (or 200g frozen peas)

1l good chicken stock at room temperature

200g carnaroli rice

1 tbsp butter

Parmesan, grated

Pasta e Zucchini

Serves 4

500g small courgettes

4 tbsp olive oil

1 garlic clove, squashed with
your hand or the blade of a
knife so it is crushed but still
in one piece

400g penne pasta

5 tbsp Pecorino cheese,
grated

zest of $\frac{1}{2}$ an unwaxed lemon

a big handful of fresh basil,
ripped into pieces

sea salt

freshly ground black pepper

*This is a great recipe for all those courgettes that grow so well in Scotland.
Choose the smallest possible; the Roman variety are best.*

Wash the courgettes and chop them into small dice (about 5mm, max). Put them on a dish towel and sprinkle with salt, then leave for 10 minutes before rinsing well.

Put 3 tablespoons of olive oil in a wide, shallow pan and heat slowly, then add the garlic and courgettes and cook for 5 minutes. Keep the heat low. Remove the garlic and discard, then continue to cook the courgettes for another 10-15 minutes until they are soft but not browned.

Meanwhile, cook the pasta in a large pot of boiling salted water until *al dente* and drain, keeping back a ladleful of the cooking water.

Put the pasta in the pan with the courgettes on a low heat, and stir in the Pecorino, grated lemon zest, basil and the saved pasta cooking water. Season with salt and freshly ground pepper to taste. After 1 minute, take the pan off the heat. Serve immediately with the remaining tablespoon of olive oil drizzled over the top.

Pasta Fagioli

Serves 4

The meat is optional, as this is equally good without.

Put the pancetta, celery, carrot and bay leaves into a large saucepan with a good 4 or 5 tablespoons of olive oil. Sweat the mixture, covered, on a medium-low heat until soft but not crisp or burnt. Put two thirds of the beans into the pot whole, then crush the remaining third in your hands as you add them. Give it all a stir, then add the tin of tomatoes, the fennel seeds and 2 ladlefuls of the water and bring up to a gentle simmer.

After 5 minutes, pour in the rest of the water and bring the pan back to the boil. Stir in the pasta and leave to simmer, but keep an eye on it. If the mixture looks like drying out at any point, add some water.

Cook until the pasta is soft – this can take a good 15 minutes. Turn off heat, season and remove the bay leaves.

2 slices good quality pancetta or, if you can find it, guanciale, diced (optional)

2 celery stalks, finely chopped

1 carrot, finely chopped

2 bay leaves

4-5 tbsp olive oil

600g mixed beans (tinned are fine, or dried, soaked and cooked)

400g tinned tomatoes

1 tbsp fennel seeds

500ml water

400g any small pasta (great for using up the left over mixed up bits in the cupboard)

sea salt

freshly ground black pepper

Pasta Cavoli

Serves 4

4 tbsp olive oil

4 garlic cloves,
finely chopped

1 tbsp fennel seeds

1 dried red chilli

100g pancetta or guanciale,
diced

1 medium cauliflower

250ml chicken or
vegetable stock

500ml water

500g any short pasta

250ml whole milk (not
skimmed or semi-skimmed)

sea salt

freshly ground black pepper

grated Pecorino and virgin
olive oil to serve

In peasant Italian cookery, pasta is cooked with every kind of brassica. Brassicas have an incredibly long growing season, from the spring cabbages to the later kale, and come in many different varieties. The cauliflower does particularly well in Scotland, making this an easy to source dish. It's very straightforward to make as it's done in one pot with the pasta cooked in the sauce. You can easily make it vegetarian by leaving out the pancetta or guanciale and using a good vegetable stock.

Put the olive oil in a large, heavy-bottomed saucepan (remember, you'll be cooking the pasta in it too) over a gentle heat. Add the garlic and leave to gently soften. Grind the fennel seeds with the chilli in a pestle and mortar and add to the pan, then stir in the pancetta or guanciale. Just keep the heat low, taking care not to brown anything, and cook gently.

Wash the cauliflower and chop it roughly, then add this to the pan and fry, stirring, for a minute or so, making sure it's well coated in the garlicky oil. Pour in the stock and water and bring to the boil, then immediately turn it down to a gentle simmer and cook, covered, for 10 minutes. Add the pasta and cook for another 5 minutes with the lid on. Then pour in the milk and continue to cook for at least 5 more minutes, stirring to stop it from sticking. The pasta should absorb almost all of the liquid, but if it looks like it's drying out before it's cooked, add a splash more water. When the pasta is very *al dente*, turn off the heat and leave it for 5 minutes, covered, so any remaining liquid is absorbed. The cauliflower will have disintegrated into a delicious, subtle sauce.

Season to taste (how much salt you need will depend on the saltiness of your stock, and whether or not you used pancetta) and serve with plenty of grated Pecorino and some virgin olive oil drizzled over.

Genovese Neapolitan

Serves 6

This Neapolitan dish is really delicious and economical. Stewing beef is one of the cheaper, tastier cuts, and cooked like this it provides two separate meals: eat the sauce with pasta and Parmesan; then serve the meat, sliced, with the remaining sauce as gravy.

In a large casserole dish, melt the butter with 2 tablespoons of olive oil over a moderate heat and seal the meat on all sides, turning it regularly to prevent sticking. Add the chopped vegetables and the apple to the pan along with the parsley and the basil, then tuck in the bay leaves and pour over the stock. Bring gently to the boil and cook, covered, on a low simmer for 1 ½ hours, stirring every so often to stop the meat sticking to the bottom. Add a splash of water if it starts to dry out.

Remove the meat on to a plate and discard the bay leaves. Using a wooden spoon, mash the vegetables into the sauce. If it's looking too thin for your liking at this stage, you can boil it down a bit. Pour in the white wine and Marsala, then put the meat back in and cook until the liquid thickens to a sauce-like consistency, coating the meat. Season to taste with sea salt and freshly ground black pepper.

At this point you can go two ways. For the pasta dish, cook some pasta – penne or ziti is best, around 100g per person. Drain when *al dente*, mix with some of the sauce and freshly grated Parmesan and cook over a low heat for a minute to bring it all together.

The meat can be served later with mashed potatoes and peas and the remaining sauce on top.

50g butter

2 tbsp olive oil

1 ½ kg onions, finely chopped

1kg stewing beef in one piece

4 carrots, roughly chopped

2 celery stalk, roughly chopped

1 small fennel bulb, roughly chopped

1 cooking apple, peeled, cored and roughly chopped

1 handful of flat-leaf parsley, chopped

2 handfuls of basil, ripped into pieces

2 bay leaves

1l good meat stock

100ml white wine

50ml Marsala

sea salt

freshly ground black pepper

Parmesan cheese to serve

Lenticchie e Salsicce

Serves 4

200g Castelluccio lentils
(or Puy, or any small brown/
green lentils)

1 garlic clove, unpeeled

1 bunch flat-leaf parsley,
washed and tied with a
piece of string

2 tbsp olive oil

1 medium onion,
finely chopped

1 stalk celery,
finely chopped

1 carrot, finely chopped

2 bay leaves

6 Italian sausages

125ml white wine

1/2 x 400g tin plum tomatoes

sea salt

freshly ground black pepper

In Italy, lentils are symbolic of money, and this dish is often eaten at New Year for luck. At Cookie we eat it all year round. Italian sausages are completely different from British sausages, and they contain no meal. We are supplied by Pietro, a Scottish-Italian who has been using the same machine and a family recipe for four generations (we sell the sausages as well). We get our lentils from Umbria, which grows the best in the world. They are similar to Puy lentils, which you can use for this recipe if you can't get your hands on an Umbrian variety such as Castelluccio.

Wash and rinse the lentils, and put them in a medium saucepan with the whole garlic clove and the bunch of parsley. Add enough water to just cover the mixture and bring it to the boil. Then simmer it, covered, until the lentils are soft but don't lose their shape (this can take anywhere from 20-40 minutes, depending on the age of your lentils). Drain the lentils over a bowl to save the cooking water, and remove the garlic and parsley.

In a large frying pan heat the olive oil, then add the onion, celery, carrot and bay leaves and cook on a low heat for 2 minutes, until everything is starting to soften. Add the whole sausages and brown them (pushing the vegetables to the side of the pan so they don't take on too much colour). Pour in the wine and cook until mostly evaporated, then add the chopped tomatoes and mix well in the pan. Let it all boil down for a minute before adding the lentils and enough of their reserved cooking water to keep the mixture liquid. Simmer until the sausages are cooked through, adding more water if it looks like it's getting too dry. Season with salt and freshly ground black pepper to taste – it may not need much in the way of salt because of the sausages.

A popular way to eat this in Italy is to serve it on the liquid side, with toasted bread to dip.

Stuffed Peppers

Serves 6 (as a side dish or starter)

These are great hot or cold and will keep in the fridge for three or four days. Pine nuts are delicious, but expensive, so you can half the quantity if need be.

Preheat the oven to 180°C.

Cut the tops off the peppers and put them to one side. Rinse the pepper cavities and clean out the seeds. In a large bowl, mix together the breadcrumbs, capers, pine nuts, Pecorino, onion, parsley and eggs and season well. The mixture should hold together when squeezed; if it's too dry, add a splash of milk.

Fill the peppers with the stuffing so they are three quarters full and put the tops back on. Stand them upright in a snug casserole dish, and then drizzle over the olive oil, the red wine vinegar and the water. Tuck the garlic cloves between the peppers and season. Then cover the casserole dish and bake for at least 1 hour. You can take the lid off the casserole for the last 10 minutes of cooking time to brown the peppers a bit on top.

6 mid-size peppers, any colour

400g breadcrumbs, from any left over stale bread

50g salted capers, rinsed

200g pine nuts

300g Pecorino cheese, grated

1 onion, finely chopped

1 bunch of flat-leaf parsley, finely chopped

4 free range eggs

3 tbsp olive oil

½ cup of red wine vinegar

200ml water

2 garlic cloves

sea salt

freshly ground black pepper

Bruno's Foccacia

1 tbsp dried yeast
(or 30g of fresh)

1 tsp sugar

350ml tepid water

500g strong white flour

1 tsp cooking salt
(don't use sea salt)

4 tbsp olive oil

extra flour for kneading

2 tbsp sea salt

20 x 30cm baking tray

This can be eaten in many different ways. It's great with our pesto on the top or with fresh rucola. You could also try scattering over some finely sliced vegetables, such as peppers, before it goes in the oven, and mixing a bit of finely chopped garlic in with the olive oil drizzled on top. Or, eat it with fresh Mozzarella di Bufala, ripe tomatoes and basil.

Preheat your oven to 190°C. Using olive oil, lightly grease your baking tray.

Reactivate the yeast: stir it and the sugar into 100ml of the water in a small jug; leave it for 15 minutes, or until a frothy head has developed.

In a large bowl, sift the flour and cooking salt, and form a well in the middle. Pour in the yeast mixture, the remaining 250ml of water and 2 tablespoons of olive oil and mix with your hands until it comes together. Then knead the dough on a floured surface for 10 minutes until it is smooth and elastic. Leave it to prove in a floured bowl, covered with a clean cloth, for an hour or so.

Once the dough has doubled in size, punch out the air, give it another 5 minute knead, and then stretch it out to a rough rectangle that fills your tin or baking tray. Leave to rise to half again in height, and then dot the dough all over with a fork, drizzle on the remaining 2 tablespoons of olive oil and scatter on the sea salt. Bake for 15 minutes and cool on a wire rack.

Torta Della Nonna

Serves 8

This special sweet tart is a bit time consuming but worth the effort for a special occasion. We use this for birthdays at Cookie, or if our chef has time on his hands!

Make the pastry first as it needs to chill for at least 2 hours. In a large metal bowl, sift the flour, icing sugar and baking powder, and then mix in the lemon zest. Rub in the cold butter until the mixture resembles fine breadcrumbs. Stir together the egg yolks, vanilla extract and honey in a small bowl, then pour the mixture into a well in the dry ingredients. Mix swiftly until the dough comes together, then wrap it in cling film and put it in the fridge for 2 hours.

When you're ready to make the torta, set the oven to 180°C. Roll the pastry out on a floured surface to a thickness of about 5mm. Line the bottom and sides of your tart tin with the pastry, and put it back in the fridge to rest while you get on with making the filling.

In a saucepan over a low heat, add 140g of the sugar to the milk and heat gently, stirring constantly. When it just starts to bubble, take it off the heat. Whisk the remaining sugar with the egg yolks and flour in a bowl, and then add the lemon zest and vanilla. Slowly pour in the hot milk, whisking all the time, and then return it all to the pan. Heat over a medium heat, stirring constantly, until the custard thickens – this will take about 5 minutes. When it's nice and thick, stir in all but a tablespoon of the pine nuts, and then pour the custard into the uncooked pastry shell. Scatter the remaining pine nuts on top and cook for 35-40 minutes, or until the filling starts to set. It will still be soft and wobbly, but it will firm up on cooling. Serve at room temperature.

Pastry

200g plain flour

70g icing sugar

½ tsp baking powder

zest of 1 unwaxed lemon, grated

85g salted butter, diced

2 large, free range egg yolks

2 drops of vanilla extract

1 tbsp honey

Filling

225g granulated sugar

450ml whole milk

4 large, free range egg yolks

55g plain flour

zest of 1 unwaxed lemon, grated

1 tsp vanilla extract

55g pine nuts

23cm loose-bottomed tart tin

Biscotti

Makes about 20

250g '00' or plain flour

200g caster sugar

1 tsp baking powder

3 free range eggs

½ a vanilla pod

1 tsp almond extract

140g hazelnuts or almonds, toasted, skinned and chopped coarsely

No Italian household is without a supply of biscotti. Traditionally left to dry out in a wood oven, they are robust biscuits. At home these are not our children's favourite, but are regarded as an "adult biscuit" which is fine by us. They make a great gift as they keep so well – just add creative packaging.

Preheat the oven to 180°C and line a baking tray with greaseproof paper.

Put the flour, sugar and baking powder in a large bowl. In another bowl, lightly beat the eggs, then scrape out the inside of the vanilla pod and add it, along with the almond extract. Stir the wet ingredients into the dry, then add the nuts and mix together into an even dough. It will be quite stiff.

Shape the dough into a long loaf shape about 8cm wide. Bake for 20 minutes until pale gold, and then remove to cool on a rack (but leave the oven on). When cool enough to handle, slice the loaf diagonally into biscuits about 1cm thick, then put the biscuits back on the baking tray and into the oven. Turn the oven off, and leave the biscuits in there overnight, or until they are crisp and dry.

Cookie Limoncello

Makes 2 litres

Limoncello, the delicious after-dinner digestif, is really easy to make. In Italy we can buy 95% alcohol specifically to make liqueurs, but this isn't an option in the UK so just use the strongest vodka you can find. We use our own, unwaxed lemons. As always, sterilise your clean jars and bottles by putting them in the dishwasher for a cycle or by giving them 10 minutes in the oven at 180°C.

This makes a lovely Christmas present.

5 unwaxed lemons

1l 50% ABV vodka

1kg caster sugar (use white sugar, not unrefined)

1l water

a large 1l airtight jar to store the steeping alcohol

Firstly, remove the zest from the lemons with a sharp knife, taking care not to include the bitter white pith. Drop the zest into the sterilised storage jar, then pour over the alcohol, seal and place in a cupboard. If you remember, you can shake it gently every few days. I never do. It will be ready in about three weeks, but longer is fine.

Once your lemon zest has steeped, make the syrup. Put the sugar and water in a pan over a medium heat and bring just to the boil, but don't let it brown at all. It will thicken up to syrup with a few minutes of simmering. Once thickened, leave the syrup to cool.

Strain the alcohol using a sieve, and add it to the syrup. Decant the mixture into sterilised bottles and it's ready. Once you have made your own, you'll never buy it again.

Melanie

We've always had a garden or allotment, so trying to make the most of all our fresh produce is part of our family cooking. At Cookie we run a barter scheme with local allotments where people can exchange their excess or interesting vegetables for coffee, lunch, etc. It's been a big success. So, this section contains many recipes that use the allotment ingredients and is mainly vegetarian as a result. If I've included bacon or guanciale, you can always leave it out. This section is heavy on baking too: we have four children so that's a lot of packed lunches needing cake. When friends visit, it's a huge number! Home baking is cheaper, and healthier, so it's a big part of my weekly routine.

Illaria's Gnocchi

Serves 4-6

1kg potatoes, weighed when peeled, then chopped into chunks
200g '00' flour
1 free range egg

Our lessons in gnocchi making came from Illaria, partner of Claudio, and owner of one of Italy's best Agritourismos, Piana Della Selve. Back in Scotland with a glut of allotment potatoes, I realised that these dumplings really should be a Scottish staple. They are a regular on the Cookie menu. While they are freezable, they don't keep well in the fridge, so try to make them just before cooking. If you do freeze them, make sure they defrost completely before cooking.

Any potato suitable for mashing will work here. The List's Larder offers a fantastic guide to all the Scottish potato varieties; if you can get them, Arran Victory are excellent.

Firstly, boil the potatoes in plenty of water (or use the classic Italian method and steam them) until tender. Next, mash them in the pan with a potato masher or, more traditionally, put them through a mouli/passa verdure or ricer. As long as they are thoroughly mashed it doesn't matter how you do it.

On a big board or a clean table top, make two piles: one of the flour, one of the cooled mash. Break the egg into a saucer and mix it lightly with a fork. Gradually mix all of the ingredients together using a bit of flour, a big handful of potatoes and a little bit of egg at a time. The idea is to mix all three ingredients as lightly as possible until it comes together into a dough – try not to overwork it. Roll your dough into three long sausages (just like the plasticine ones you made in primary one). Dust each sausage with flour, then cut each one into 1cm chunks. The dough cuts with a butter knife, so this is quite a nice job for kids and makes them feel important. You can press each gnocchi against a fine cheese grater for a perfect finish, or leave them rough if you prefer. Put them on a plate, well-dusted with flour so they don't stick together.

Gnocchi couldn't be simpler to cook, but ideally you should do it as soon as possible once they are made. Bring a big pan of salted water to a rolling boil, then turn the heat down to medium and drop in the gnocchi, one at a time, in batches of six or so. They are cooked when they float up to the surface, which will take about a minute. Remove them with a slotted spoon onto a serving plate and keep them warm.

They are best eaten with a simple tomato sauce (like the one on page 79) and cheese.

Gnocchi with Squash

Serves 4-6

1kg squash of your choice
(all varieties are good)

2 garlic cloves,
finely chopped

3 tbsp olive oil

2 free range eggs

200g '00' flour

100g ground almonds

50g Pecorino, grated

sea salt

If you liked the potato gnocchi recipe and have seen how easy it is to make, try these for a seasonal variation. They're great for children as they cook very quickly. They are an autumn favourite at Cookie, and a family tradition at Halloween.

Firstly, heat the oven to 190°C. Cut the squash into chunks and toss with the garlic onto a large roasting tray. Drizzle the squash with olive oil, sprinkle on some sea salt and roast for about 45 minutes until soft but not brown. While it's still hot, scrape the contents of the roasting tray into a large bowl and mash with a potato masher.

The next bit can be done in a mixer with a dough hook, or very thoroughly by hand. Add all of the remaining ingredients to the mashed squash and mix well until you have a smooth mixture. It will be quite runny, but the gnocchi will firm up when you boil them.

When you're ready to cook, fill a large pan with salted water, bring it to the boil and then drop in heaped teaspoons of the mixture (you can probably have five or so cooking at any one time). They're ready when they float to the surface of the water, which will only take a minute or so. Remove the gnocchi with a slotted spoon and place them on a warm serving dish.

We serve this with sage butter, or simply with some Parmesan and a drizzle of good olive oil.

Sage Butter

50g butter

about 15 sage leaves, finely chopped

2 tbsp olive oil

Melt the butter in a pan, but don't allow it to brown. Add the chopped leaves and cook for a few minutes on low, again avoiding any crisping or burning. Turn off the heat and add the olive oil.

Ragù

This is a great, big quantity dish which freezes well and can be used in a whole variety of ways, not just with pasta. It is particularly good with polenta or on bruschetta.

Melt the butter and a tablespoon of oil in a large shallow pan, then add the beef and the pork and brown on a medium heat, stirring all the time to stop it sticking. Take the pan off the heat, pour in the red wine and Marsala and leave to one side.

Heat the other tablespoon of olive oil in a heavy-bottomed casserole. Put in the bay leaf, carrots, celery and the onion and cook gently until soft but not brown. Add the meat and juices to the dish, mix them together and then stir in the tomatoes and a spoonful of tomato puree. Using the empty tomato tin, add about two tins of water – the meat should be just covered by liquid.

Scatter in the freshly grated nutmeg and, once you've got it all boiling, reduce the heat to a gentle simmer. Leave to the ragù to cook, covered, on a very low heat for 1½-2 hours – it should be just trembling, not boiling.

Serve with pasta, polenta, potatoes, or whatever you feel like.

50g butter

2 tbsp olive oil

250g braising beef, minced or diced

250g pork, minced or diced

100ml red wine

50ml Marsala

1 bay leaf

2 carrots, finely chopped

2 celery stalks, finely chopped

1 onion, finely chopped

400g tinned tomatoes

1 tbsp tomato puree

1 tsp nutmeg, freshly grated

sea salt

Polenta

Serves 4

1.8l water
1 tsp salt
300g polenta

Though polenta itself was introduced to Italy in the 17th century, polenta-like dishes made with spelt or buckwheat were probably being eaten for centuries before. It's a classic poor man's food with a wide range of culinary possibilities. There are many different varieties, from fine to coarse, and from rich yellow to the white variety from the Veneto.

Think of slightly wet, soft polenta as a good alternative to mash; it goes well with ragùs and even fish stews, or really any sauce-based dish. Alternatively, enjoy it plain with butter or cheese. Left overnight to firm up, polenta makes a great base for canapes: simply cut small pieces and top them with something interesting. The cooked and cooled firm version is also good fried or grilled.

There are several quick-cook polentas available, and the cooking time and method will be on the packet. If you are cooking it the traditional way, you will need a big wide-bottomed saucepan and a long-handled wooden spoon as polenta needs to be stirred but spits while cooking.

Bring the water to the boil and add the salt. Take the pan off the heat. Put the dry polenta into a jug, and pour it into the water in a steady stream, whisking all the time. I use a balloon whisk for this, which is possibly not traditional but works well. When the polenta is well mixed with no lumps, put the pan back on a medium heat. Bring it back up to the boil, stirring all the time with your long-handled wooden spoon. Boil gently for 10 minutes, then turn the heat right down and simmer gently, stirring every now and then, for another 15 minutes.

Ribollita

Serves 4-6

My first few years of allotment gardening in Scotland did not yield bumper crops. However, I did get enough to make this soup which, due to the right mix of vegetables, was a great way to serve my small misshapen offerings. Thanks to our barter scheme with local allotment growers, we often have some fantastic things to put in this dish that would be harder to source commercially – Glasgow-grown cavolo nero is particularly good. The quantities below can be varied according to what's in season and available.

This is a slow-cook soup, but it's such a meal in itself that it's well worth the wait. The name comes from the Italian for 'reboiled', as it was traditionally made using left over vegetable soup finished off in the oven.

Heat the oil gently in the base of a large soup pot, then put in the onion, celery and guanciale and cook until everything is soft but not browned. Add the potatoes, cover and sweat for 3 minutes, making sure nothing burns. Next, pour in the tins of tomatoes and the beans, crumble in the thyme leaves and add 2 litres of water. Bring to the boil, then turn to down to a slow simmer and cover. After an hour, add the cavolo nero and continue to simmer, still covered, for one hour more. Make sure it's not drying out or sticking and add more water if required. It will be a thick soup, but it should be like soup nonetheless. Season to taste with salt and pepper.

When the soup is cooked, heat the oven to 180°C. Line the bottom of an oven-proof casserole dish with the slices of bread (cut them at least 1cm thick – you need a bit of body to them) and pour the soup over.

Put in the oven, uncovered, for another 15 minutes, and then serve with a drizzle of olive oil.

3 tbsp olive oil

1 onion, finely chopped

1 stalk celery, finely chopped

2 slices guanciale (or pancetta if not available), finely chopped

2 potatoes, peeled and diced

2 x 400g tins Italian tomatoes

2 x 400g tins cannellini beans (or 150g dried beans soaked overnight and drained)

1 sprig of thyme, leaves only

700g cavolo nero, shredded

4 slices sourdough or other good bread

sea salt

freshly ground black pepper

extra olive oil to serve

Asparagus Risotto

Serves 4

500g asparagus

1l good chicken stock

100g unsalted butter

3 tbsp olive oil

½ a white onion,
finely chopped

250g arborio rice

500ml white wine

½ tbsp flat-leaf parsley,
finely chopped

50g Parmesan, grated

sea salt

freshly ground black pepper

Though British asparagus is fantastic, I've had no success growing it in Scotland. We do manage to get a huge crop on our hill in Italy, but this truly has nothing to do with me – it's just wild. The Italian variety is thinner and purple, and it has as good a taste as the British variety. Choosing to cook seasonally makes asparagus worthwhile, as it's inexpensive when in season (or free if we are in Italy). Asparagus has a relatively short season – spring or summer depending on the local climate. Imported, out of season asparagus is over-priced, generally slightly wilted and usually tasteless.

There are several really great ways to enjoy asparagus – one of my favourites is with a soft boiled egg, using the stalks to dip. A risotto, however, really makes the most of it, especially if you don't have very much. A small supply can make this beautifully coloured and distinctively tasty dish.

Cut the tips off the asparagus and roughly chop the stalks into 2cm pieces. Put the tips to one side. In a saucepan, bring the stock to a simmer and check for seasoning.

In a wide, thick-bottomed pan, melt 50g butter and all of the olive oil. Add the onion and cook gently until soft. Put in the rice and stir to coat each grain, cooking gently until they just turn translucent. Add the asparagus stalks and stir, then pour in the wine and let it bubble until reduced by half.

Start to add the hot stock, ladleful by ladleful, only adding more when the last amount has been absorbed. Keep stirring and continue to add the stock until the rice is cooked (around 20 minutes in total). You may not need all of the stock. After about 15 minutes of cooking the rice, add the reserved asparagus tips, as they will cook quickly.

Once the rice is cooked, remove the pan from the heat and stir in the remaining butter along with the parsley and Parmesan.

Serve with a good drizzle of olive oil and extra Parmesan.

Roast Chicken

Serves 4-6

Surely this is one of the best meals on the planet. After spending so much time in Italy, I've gone over to the Italian way of roasting the bird; it's quicker, and I like the flavours better. As ever, buy the best chicken you can, for all the right reasons. Either get your butcher to cut it into pieces or do it yourself. The smaller the pieces, the quicker the roasting time – I usually cut it into two legs, four pieces of breast and two wings. If you don't fancy jointing it completely, simply cut it in half down the breastbone, and make some large scores with a knife into the skin.

Preheat the oven to 190°C.

Put the potato pieces in a large roasting tray with the whole cloves of garlic and season well. Then scatter over half the crushed garlic and all of the rosemary and thyme. Drizzle with 2 tablespoons of the olive oil and mix with your hands, making sure all the pieces are well coated. Lay the chicken on top, skin side up. Sprinkle the remaining garlic over the chicken, and then drizzle the whole lot with the remaining 2 tablespoons of oil. Squeeze over the lemon juice and then put the tray in the oven.

It will need around 35-45 minutes to cook: it's done when the juices run clear from the chicken pieces if pierced, and the potatoes are golden brown but soft enough to stick a skewer through. I usually take the tray out after 20 minutes and mix everything really well with a big long-handled spoon, and then return it to the oven for the rest of the cooking time.

Serve with the lemons for squeezing over and some sea salt.

6 potatoes, unpeeled and cut into quarters

8 garlic cloves (4 peeled and crushed slightly, and 4 left whole)

2 tbsp fresh rosemary, finely chopped

2 tbsp thyme, finely chopped

4 tbsp olive oil

1 whole free range chicken, jointed

juice of 1/2 a lemon

sea salt

freshly ground black pepper

2 lemons, quartered, to serve

Asparagus Frittata

Serves 4

6 eggs

50g pecorino, grated

25g butter

3 tbsp olive oil

½ onion, finely sliced

500g asparagus, cut diagonally into 1cm pieces

sea salt

freshly ground black pepper

Another way to enjoy your asparagus. Cookie serves frittata regularly as it is versatile and fresh. At home we will use any leftovers as lunch the next day with salad; it's often even better. I do this with two separate pans, but it's easy enough to use one and clean it mid-recipe. For the frittata you need a large-ish frying pan.

First break the eggs into a bowl, add the pecorino and season with black pepper and a pinch of salt. Don't whisk them, just gently mix with a fork to break up the yolk.

Heat a tablespoon of olive oil and half the butter gently in a pan and soften the onion. Add the asparagus after 3 minutes and cook gently for another 3 minutes. Turn off the heat, leave to cool for a minute or two and then stir the mixture into the eggs.

Heat the remaining oil and butter in your frittata pan on medium high until the butter melts. Pour in the egg mixture and immediately turn the heat down to medium, then cover with a large plate, one that is a good bit bigger than the pan. Cook for 2 to 3 minutes, until the eggs are beginning to firm up on the bottom. Take the pan off the heat and, with one hand holding the plate firmly in place, turn the whole lot upside down so the fritatta ends up uncooked-side down on the plate. Put the pan back on the heat and slide the frittata back in – you will have some runny egg left on the plate as well, but just add it in. Don't stir, try to keep it all in one piece. Cook for 1-2 minutes, until golden on both sides, and serve.

Alternatively, if your chosen frying pan is ovenproof and you don't have a suitable plate/pan combination, you can put it in the oven at 180°C for 5 minutes once the bottom side of the frittata is cooked, taking it out when the top is set, puffy and golden.

Arnold Bennett Omelette

Serves 2 (or one greedy person)

Ahhh, the omelette! Loved by family and Cookie for its versatility and freshness, this was originally cooked for the writer Arnold Bennett at his request when staying in the London Savoy. It became his signature dish and remains on their menu. With our good supply of smoked haddock, it's a great easy meal in Scotland. It's simple and, although (unlike Arnold Bennett) you might not want it every time you eat out, it does have a certain addictive quality. This recipe uses a large (30cm or so) frying pan, non-stick if you have it, that can go under the grill.

Place the fish in a wide, shallow pan and pour on the milk. Add the bay leaf and the peppercorns. Bring the mixture slowly to a simmer and cook gently for 10 minutes, but don't overcook the fish. Drain into a colander over a bowl to reserve the milk, and take out the bay and the peppercorns. Flake the fish onto a plate, leaving it in good sized pieces and discarding any bones or bits of skin.

In a heavy-bottomed pan, melt 30g of the butter slowly. As soon as it has melted, stir in the flour and allow it to cook a little until it smells of biscuits and goes the colour of straw. Make sure the heat stays low. Then, beating all the time, slowly add the reserved fishy milk to make a smooth white sauce. Keep stirring over a medium-low heat until it starts to thicken, then add the cream. You are aiming for a sauce that's thick but not too solid. Leave it to one side.

Gently stir the flaked fish into the eggs. Melt the remaining butter in a large, non-stick or cast iron frying pan over a medium heat, and then pour in the fish and egg mix in one go. Shake the pan to spread the omelette

200g smoked haddock

200ml whole milk

1 bay leaf

3 whole black peppercorns

60g butter

3 tbsp plain flour

50ml double cream

6 free range eggs, lightly beaten

50g Pecorino, grated

sea salt

freshly ground black pepper

evenly, then immediately turn the heat down to low and cook for 6 minutes or so until the eggs are firming up. Pour the white sauce over the top, sprinkle with the grated cheese and put under the grill until golden brown and bubbling. The omelette will rise slightly.

Note: It's not the professional way, but I use a hand-blender on very low to finish a white sauce. Technology has its place and no one complains about a lack of lumps.

Melanie's Oatmeal and Honey Bread

With oatmeal, a fantastic cholestrol-lowerer, and honey to boost immunity, this is my winter breakfast bread.

Grease your loaf tin. Activate your yeast as usual: put it into a small jug with the sugar and 100ml of the tepid water, give it a quick stir and leave it for 15 minutes or so. Once it develops a frothy head, it's ready.

Put the flour and oatmeal into a large bowl and rub in the butter. Add the salt, and then pour in the yeasty water, the milk, the remaining 100ml of tepid water and the honey, and mix it with your hands until it comes together as a dough. Turn it out onto a floured surface, knead for 10 minutes (or 5 in a mixer) until it's smooth and elastic, and then put it in a floured bowl covered with a cloth to rise. After an hour or so it will have doubled in size, so punch it down, give it another 5 minute knead and put it into your greased tin.

At this point, turn your oven on to 200°C. Meanwhile, leave your dough to double in size (about 30 minutes).

Slash the top three times and sprinkle it with flour. Bake the dough for 10 minutes, and then turn the heat down to 190°C and bake for a further 20 minutes. Turn the loaf out onto a wire rack and leave it to cool.

1 tbsp dried yeast (or 30g of fresh)

1 tsp sugar

200ml tepid water

400g strong white bread flour

100g medium oatmeal

1 tbsp butter

1 tsp cooking salt (not sea salt)

150ml lukewarm milk

1 tbsp honey (thick honey will melt with the warm water but runny mixes easier)

extra flour for kneading

900g loaf tin

Walnut and Seed Bread

400ml tepid water

1 tsp sugar

1 tbsp dried yeast (or 30g of fresh)

150g strong wholemeal flour

350g strong white flour

1 tsp cooking salt (not sea salt)

50g walnuts, toasted in a dry pan for 5 minutes, then roughly chopped

100g mixed seeds

1 tbsp walnut oil (or olive oil if unavailable)

extra flour for kneading

This is great with savouries and cheese. Use any type of seeds you like: we use a mixture of pumpkin, sesame and sunflower. Somehow, this tastes best baked as a free-standing loaf, not in a tin.

First, activate your yeast by putting 100ml of the tepid water in a small measuring jug and adding the sugar and yeast. Give it a quick stir with a fork and leave for 10-15 minutes until a frothy head has formed.

Put both flours into a large bowl with the salt, the chopped walnuts and the seeds. Make a well in the middle and pour in the yeasty liquid, the remaining 300ml of water and the oil. Stir quickly until it comes together as a dough, then turn out onto a floured board and knead it thoroughly for 10 minutes or so, until the dough becomes smooth and elastic (5 minutes in a mixer with a dough hook will do). Put the dough into a floured bowl covered with a clean tea towel and leave to rise. Once the dough has doubled in size (about an hour later), punch it down and knead it again for another 5 minutes (or 3 in a mixer). Form the dough into a round loaf, smoothing the surface with wet hands, and put it onto a floured baking tray. Cover the loaf with a tea towel and leave it to double in size (for about 30 minutes). While the dough is rising again, preheat the oven to 190°C.

Once the loaf has doubled in size, sprinkle the top with a handful of flour, and slash it three times with a sharp knife. Bake it for 25 minutes and then cool on a wire rack. You'll know it's done baking if it sounds hollow when you tap on the base.

Rhubarb (or Whatever-the-Garden-Provided) Crumble

Serves 4-6

There are many variations on a crumble, and you can use any fruit that's in season. At Cookie we start serving crumble towards the end of summer, when the apples are getting ripe. Our absolute favourites are: rhubarb, apple, apple and bramble (you only need about 20 brambles for a rich purple crumble), rhubarb and ginger, and gooseberry.

Preheat the oven to 200°C.

Prepare your fruit: for apple crumble, peel and dice the apples; for rhubarb crumble, chop the rhubarb into 1cm pieces. Stew the fruit of your choice in a pan with a teaspoon of sugar and enough water to come up the fruit about a quarter of the way. If you're using rhubarb, add a tablespoon or orange juice to the pan. Simmer the fruit until it's soft, and then pour it into an oven-proof dish.

To make the crumble, put the oats and flour in a large bowl and then stir in the sugar and any relevant spices. With your fingertips, rub in the butter until the mixture resembles fine breadcrumbs. Spread the crumble in a layer over the fruit and bake it for about 30 minutes, or until the top is crisp and the fruit is bubbling around the edges. Serve with crème fraîche, cream, yoghurt or ice cream.

1kg fruit

1 tsp caster sugar

80g oats

100g '00' or plain flour

100g demerara sugar

for apple crumble, add a pinch of cinnamon, $\frac{1}{4}$tsp freshly grated nutmeg and a pinch of cloves

for rhubarb crumble, add a pinch of ground ginger

80g unsalted butter, diced

Beetroot and Chocolate Cake

Serves 8-10

Cake

50g cocoa

6 tbsp boiling water

175g '00' or plain flour

½ tsp bicarbonate of soda

1 ½ tsp baking powder

225g caster sugar

115g butter, very soft

3 free range eggs

5 tbsp milk

1 tsp vanilla extract

225g raw beetroot, grated

80g chocolate (at least 60% cocoa solids), chopped into small pieces

65g walnuts (optional)

Icing

400g icing sugar

100g plain chocolate (at least 70% cocoa solids), melted

100g butter, melted

2 x 20cm round cake tins

This is a great cake. It's not recognisable as beetroot cake – only as very intense chocolate cake. It's lower in fat than most chocolate cakes, and the beetroot is a great antioxidant and, supposedly, a liver stimulant. The cake also freezes well. The only work in this recipe is grating the beetroot; I've tried it with cooked beetroot, and it doesn't work. If you don't have a food processor, enlist a helper of the type who finds purple hands amusing. If not, wear gloves.

Preheat oven to 180°C. Grease and line the cake tins.

In a small bowl, make a paste with the cocoa and the boiling water. In another bowl, sift together the flour, bicarbonate of soda and baking powder. In a third bowl, mix together with an electric whisk the sugar, butter, eggs, milk and vanilla extract, and then add the cocoa paste. Fold in the dry ingredients, and then quickly but thoroughly stir in the grated beetroot, the chocolate and the walnuts (if you're using them).

Pour the batter into your prepared tins and bake in the oven for 30 minutes, or until a skewer in the middle comes out without any mixture sticking to it.

Due to its healthiness, this cake deserves to be smothered in fat-laden chocolate icing. Sift the icing sugar into a bowl, and mix with the melted chocolate and butter. Whisk the icing until it's stiff but spreadable - you'll have enough to sandwich the two cakes together and ice the top. If you can't be bothered, you can just stick the cakes together with strawberry or apricot jam and it will still be delicious.

Spiced Parsnip Cake

Serves 8-10

We first used this recipe for a kids' class on cooking with vegetables. As far as I can tell, it originated from wartime when dairy products were scarce and shortages led to great inventiveness. Parsnips are easy to grow (our allotment does loads here in Glasgow) and cheap to buy, and they make a really lovely textured cake. It's a firm Cookie favourite every autumn.

Preheat the oven to 180°C and grease and line your cake tin.

Peel the parsnips and remove the hard core. Chop them into 1cm dice and put them into a small pan with the water. Simmer gently until they are very soft and then, without draining, purée with a hand-blender until smooth. Leave to cool, and then stir in the bicarbonate of soda.

In a large bowl, cream the butter, sugar and vanilla until light and fluffy, and then add the eggs one at a time, beating well between each one. Fold in the flour and spices, then the raisins, and then the parsnip purée. Finally, stir in the milk to make a nice dropping consistency. Pour the batter into the prepared tin and bake for 45-60 minutes, until it's golden brown and a skewer in the middle comes out clean. Cool on a wire rack.

At Cookie we don't ice this cake – we just make a really simple glaze to go on the top. Simply heat half a jar of apricot jam until runny (but not boiling), and strain it through a sieve onto the cake.

300g parsnip, weighed when peeled and cored

250ml water

1 tsp bicarbonate of soda

100g butter, softened

175g soft brown sugar (or caster sugar will do)

1 tsp vanilla extract (or the scraped insides of a quarter of a vanilla pod)

2 free range eggs

300g self-raising flour

1 tsp mixed spice

1 tsp ground ginger

2 tsp nutmeg

80g raisins

3 tbsp milk

1/2 jar apricot jam (optional)

Courgette Cake

Serves 8-10

2 free range eggs

125ml vegetable oil (we use our olive oil)

160g caster sugar

225g self-raising flour

½ tsp bicarbonate of soda

½ tsp baking powder

250g courgettes, grated with skins on

Healthier than carrot cake, this courgette cake is really quick to make. Glasgow allotments are full of courgettes all summer, and most gardeners will tell you they have a glut of them, so courgette recipes are always welcome. And like any vegetable cake, it's great for kids.

We bake this just like a Victoria sponge and sandwich two cakes together: either bake it in two 20cm cake tins, or make one larger cake and split it once it's cooled. It's good with cream cheese in the middle, or fresh cream and fruit, but what you do with it is up to you.

Preheat the oven to 180°C and grease and line your cake tin(s). In a large bowl, beat the eggs, oil and sugar together with a whisk. Sieve in the flour, bicarbonate of soda and baking powder and fold together swiftly. Then fold in the courgettes and pour the batter into the prepared tin(s). It's that simple.

Two small tins will take about 30 minutes to bake, a bigger tin about 40, but it does depend on your oven. There's lots written about baking and how much of an exact science it is: don't open the oven mid-cooking, make sure everything is perfect, etc. These recipes are for family. In my experience, just cook it until you can stick a skewer into the middle without getting any sticky uncooked bits on it, and you are done. If you leave the oven open for ages while you prod it and try to decide if it's done, the worst thing that can happen is that it sinks a bit. So what? You learn to be quicker with the skewer next time, or not to bother. Just put more filling in the middle. It will taste good anyway.

Grandma Christine

Grandma Christine is from the highlands of Scotland, one of the most amazing parts of the country from a culinary point of view. There's also the generational aspect: hers was a generation before packaged foods, when people really cooked and everything was made to last as long and stretch as far as possible. She has cooked everything from scratch, for a large family, forever. She's always in the kitchen and always ready to cook for hordes of visitors.

We grew up in a fairly remote part of Scotland, so the most available products were local and seasonal. Imported items were a rare luxury. This section of the book has a really Scottish feel to it – in Cookie we have a regular supply of seasonal game, as well as the best Scottish fish and cheese we can find. We are active in our endeavours to bring these items back into everyone's kitchens and off the lorries which go straight to France and Spain.

Smoked Mackerel Pâté

Serves 4-6

3 smoked mackerel fillets

150g ricotta cheese

100g creme fraîche

4 tsp fresh horseradish, grated

lemon juice

freshly ground black pepper

Scottish fish were traditionally smoked to preserve them – the flavour was an added bonus. We are lucky to have fantastic mackerel, a cheap and plentiful fish at the moment.

Smoking your own fish can be fun, but equally we have several excellent quality smokehouses which supply us. Our horseradish comes from the allotment where it grows happily and without much encouragement. Together, they make a great pâté – simple and full of flavour.

Skin the mackerel and remove any bones. Place in a food processor and whizz with the ricotta, creme fraîche and horseradish. Add a good grind of black pepper and lemon juice to taste. This pâté is fantastic on rye bread.

Venison MacDuff

Serves 4

Roe deer and red deer are native to Scotland and have been roaming the Highlands for at least 10,000 years. Cookie regularly has a good supply of wild venison. The quality of the meat begins with the hunt and depends on efficient butchery and immediate cold storage. Venison is a low fat meat and is also very low in cholesterol. However, whatever fat there is on the animal has a bad taste, so it's important to remove all of it prior to cooking. This necessitates using other fats when cooking, such as butter or bacon. Never salt venison, never overcook it, and try to choose a method of cooking that adds moisture, such as this slow cook stew with cranberries.

Put the venison in a large freezer bag with the flour and give it a good shake to coat the meat. Heat the butter and oil in a large, heavy casserole and brown the meat in batches, removing it to a plate as it's done. Turn the heat down low and put in the onions and bacon, and cook slowly until they're soft but not at all brown. Add a splash more oil if it looks like anything is sticking. Add the mushrooms and cook for another 5 minutes or so. Return the meat to the pan along with any juices that have collected on the plate, and then pour over the wine and the stock. Stir in the rowan jelly, the bay leaf, the nutmeg and the thyme. Bring the mixture up to a boil, stir it, and then immediately turn down the heat and simmer it, covered, for an hour. Add the cranberries and cook for a further hour with the lid off. Keep an eye on it to make sure it doesn't dry out, and add a bit more water if needed. Season the stew just before serving. It's great with mash.

1kg venison, diced

2 tbsp flour

50g butter

1 tbsp olive oil

1 onion, finely chopped

100g bacon or guanciale, diced

100g mushrooms (either whole baby mushrooms or regular ones) chopped

1/4 bottle red wine

200ml good beef stock

1 1/2 tbsp rowan and crab apple jelly (see page 64, or redcurrant will do)

1 bay leaf

1/4 nutmeg, freshly grated

1 sprig of fresh thyme, leaves only

110g fresh cranberries

sea salt

freshly ground black pepper

Roast Pheasant with Italian Sausage Stuffing

Serves 4 - 6

200g Italian sausage

½ an onion, finely chopped

1 tbsp flat-leaf parsley, fincly chopped

30g fresh breadcrumbs

1 free range egg, lightly beaten

2 pheasants, prepared

50g butter

6 rashers streaky bacon

2 tbsp rowan and crab apple jelly (see page 64, or use redcurrant jelly)

½ bottle red wine

juice of 1 lemon

sea salt

freshly ground black pepper

All families have their funny stories relating to food. We still laugh about the dark winter evening when our visiting city cousins came in through the utility room and screamed loud enough to make us think murder had occurred in the sleepy Highlands. The cause? A gift of several pheasants from the local gamekeeper, hanging up ready for my mother.

Pheasant is much cheaper than you would imagine, and a whole bird is plenty for two people. It is possible, these days, to buy just the breast, but we like to use the whole bird and make the most of this wonderful Scottish game.

Preheat the oven to 180°C.

Firstly, make the stuffing. Remove the skin from the sausage and put the meat in a bowl. With your hands, mash the sausage meat with the onion, parsley, and breadcrumbs, and then mix in about half the beaten egg and season well. You can discard the rest of the egg, or use it to glaze some of Elliot's bread rolls (see page 122). Now to stuff your birds: slide your fingers gently under the skin of the breast to loosen it from the flesh, and then push in the stuffing in an even layer. Repeat for the second bird. Make little balls about the size of a walnut out of any left-overs, as these can be cooked alongside the pheasant.

Put the birds in a greased roasting pan and rub them all over with butter. Cover the breasts with streaky bacon and roast for 30 minutes. Take the birds out of the oven and baste with the fat which has drained off, and then leave them to cool for a few minutes. When they're cool enough to handle, brush the jelly over the legs and breast, pour over the wine and the lemon juice and season lightly. Return to the oven for another 30 minutes, or until the juices run clear when poked with a skewer.

When they're done, put the birds on a serving dish and keep them warm while you make the gravy. Strain the liquid from the roasting pan and reduce it by boiling hard in a small pan for 5 minutes, until you have a rich, thick gravy.

Clapshot

Serves 4

*500g floury potatoes,
peeled and diced*

*500g swede/large turnips,
peeled and diced*

50g butter

*50ml double cream
(optional)*

Clapshot originated from Orkney and is basically the neeps in "neeps 'n' tatties". There are two ways to do this: the foolproof method is to use two pans and cook the potatoes and swede separately; or you can just use one pan, which means less washing up, but you have to be sure when to add the potatoes!

Bring two pans of water to the boil, and cook both vegetables until just soft. If you're using just one pan, make sure everything is cut into even dice, and add the potato when the swede has been boiling for about 4 minutes.

Drain the vegetables, mash them together with the butter, and add the cream (if using). Season the clapshot well and serve.

Red Cabbage

Serves 8-10

This is a versatile vegetable, a great accompaniment to any slow cooked meats and fantastic with venison. At Cookie, we like to cook the cabbage really slowly, allowing the flavours to develop. This makes a lot, but it is very popular and freezes well. You will need a large, heavy based casserole that can go in the oven.

Preheat the oven to 140°C.

Lightly grease the casserole and put about a third of the cabbage in the bottom. Scatter over half of the apples, half of the onion, half of the garlic, 1 teaspoon of brown sugar, 1 teaspoon of salt, 2 juniper berries and roughly half the butter. Try to scatter these ingredients over the cabbage in an even layer. Then add another third of the grated cabbage, and repeat. Finish with a layer of cabbage. Pour over the vinegar. Don't stir, just cover the dish and put it in the oven. After about an hour, you can stir the mixture and then return it to the oven for another hour. If it's drying out at all, add a small amount of water.

Finish with a tablespoon of butter stirred through just before serving.

1 red cabbage, finely grated

2 Bramley apples, peeled, cored and finely chopped

½ an onion, finely chopped

1 garlic clove, finely chopped

2 tsp soft brown sugar

2 tsp sea salt

4 juniper berries

50g butter cut into 1cm dice, plus 1 tbsp to serve

75ml balsamic vinegar

Cookie Cabbage

Serves 8

2 tbsp olive oil

1 onion, thinly sliced

1 small slice guanciale or pancetta, diced

1 small garlic clove, finely chopped

4 carrots, grated

1 large savoy cabbage, grated or shredded

100ml water

1 tbsp butter

sea salt

freshly ground black pepper

A good accompaniment to roast dinners, or to many of Cookie's slow cooked meats like Venison MacDuff (page 53), British cabbages are wonderful, and we have found they taste great combined with a small amount of guanciale.

We always called this dish Bubble and Squeak; however, on researching for the cookbook I discovered that Bubble and Squeak is actually an English leftovers dish. But whatever it's called, it's still on our menu.

Heat the oil in a large, shallow pan, and add the onion, guanciale and garlic and cook over a medium-low heat until soft. Throw in the grated carrots and the cabbage and fry for 5 minutes, stirring from time to time. Pour in the water and bring to the boil, then cover and immediately reduce the heat to a gentle simmer. Cook the mixture for 6 minutes, adding a splash more water if it looks like it's drying out before the vegetables are soft.

When the cabbage and carrots are tender and the liquid absorbed, season, stir in the butter and serve.

Clootie Dumpling (Clootie, from the Scots meaning a rag or cloth)

Serves 6-8

The clootie and the Christmas pudding share a similar origin dating back to the 15th century, a time when the lack of animal food forced the culling of animals at the end of autumn. One way of preserving the meat for longer was to make a dumpling: a big mix of meat, sugar and dried fruit, boiled slowly in a cloth bag. Nowadays, we use the dumpling more as a sweet.

In the Black Isle of Scotland, if you are really lucky you may come across the travelling people's clootie trees: pieces of rag, supposedly that have been worn by someone ill, are tied to the tree, and the drying of them brings that person back to good health. Although they're not really in the spirit of today's public health measures, the clootie trees are a good reminder that folklore continues to thrive in parts of Scotland.

It comes as no surprise that this Scottish dumpling can be recycled into a breakfast. When accompanied by some Ayrshire bacon, it will sort out the previous evening with Souter Johnny or any other drouthy crony.

2 free range eggs

1 tbsp golden syrup

140ml milk

110g suet

220g self-raising flour, plus extra for dusting

1 tsp baking powder

110g breadcrumbs

85g soft brown sugar

1 tsp cinnamon

1 tsp ground ginger

1 tsp grated nutmeg

1 cooking apple, grated

110g currants

110g sultanas

A large muslin or cheesecloth

string

Put an inverted plate on the bottom of a large pot and half fill the pot with water. Bring it to the boil. Soak a muslin or cheese cloth in the water and then squeeze it out and lay it flat on a work surface before dusting it with flour.

In a small bowl, beat the eggs with a bulging teaspoon of golden syrup and the milk. Put the rest of the ingredients into a separate bowl and pour the egg mixture in, stirring, to get a stiff-ish batter. Dump this into the middle of the cloth, and then bring the corners of the cloth up and tie them tightly with string just above the pudding, but leave room for swelling.

Put the pudding on top of the plate in the pot and boil for 3 hours, making sure the water always comes at least half way up the pudding. After 3 hours, drain the water out of the pot, dip the pudding quickly in some cold water, then peel off the cloth and invert the pudding onto an ovenproof dish. Dry it off in the oven at around 160°C for 20 minutes and serve with custard (see page 103).

Scones

Makes 8-10

225g self-raising flour

40g butter, softened

1½ tbsp caster sugar

a pinch of fine salt

150ml whole milk

plain flour for kneading and dusting

7cm cutter or glass

Scones are a Highland speciality. They're relatively cheap to make and actually pretty low in fat, probably a lot like the original Highland diet. Cookie always has fresh scones to go with our jams.

Preheat the oven to 220°C. Lightly grease a baking sheet.

Sift the flour into a bowl. Rub in the butter with your fingertips, as quickly as possible. Stir in the sugar and the salt, and then stir in the milk with a butter knife. Using the knife and then your hands, draw the dough into a ball.

Rub a tablespoon of plain flour onto your hands, pick up the dough and turn it onto a floured work surface. It's important not to knead your dough; just lightly smooth it with a rolling pin to about 3cm high. Put your cutter on the dough and press it down sharply (don't twist it) to cut out the scones. Press out as many as you can, then draw the left over dough together as quickly and simply as possible and repeat until you have used it all up.

Put the scones on the prepared baking sheet and lightly sprinkle each one with flour. Bake them in the oven for 12-15 minutes, until they're risen and golden. Cool the scones on a wire tray and eat them as soon as possible, although they do freeze well.

Marmalade and Chocolate Cake

Serves 8-10

This recipe comes from our great friend and cook, Gail Rainey. She had several unsuccessful attempts at a chocolate orange cake from Nigella Lawson's How to Be a Domestic Goddess. Like a true goddess, she rejigged it a bit and now it's easy. It's in this section as Grandma is our marmalade expert.

Marmalade oranges are generally in season from January to early February. The marmalade will keep for ages, so you can make this cake any time of the year, but we like to keep to the seasons as a reference for what we eat so we generally have this in February.

Preheat the oven to 180°C. Grease and line a 20cm tin (or a loaf tin, if you like).

Empty the marmalade into a small bowl and stir in the bicarbonate of soda. In a bowl big enough to take all of the ingredients, melt the butter and chocolate over boiling water or in the microwave on low heat. Add the marmalade mixture, the sugar and the eggs, and beat well. Fold in the flour. Pour the batter into your prepared tin and bake for 40 minutes, or until a skewer poked in the middle comes out clean. Turn out the cake and cool on a rack. This is best eaten as it is, without icing.

340g marmalade (see page 67)

½ tsp bicarbonate of soda

125g butter

150g chocolate (70% cocoa solids)

150g caster sugar

3 free range eggs

150g self-raising flour

20cm cake tin

Oatcakes

Makes 18-20

175g wholemeal flour

50g medium oatmeal

3 tsp soft brown sugar

1 tsp baking powder

½ tsp salt

¼ tsp curry powder

110g unsalted butter

1 tbsp milk

7cm cutter or glass

Preheat the oven to 180°C, and lightly grease a baking sheet.

Mix all the dry ingredients together, and then rub in the butter with your fingertips until it's the texture of breadcrumbs. Add the milk, pulling the mixture together with your hands at the same time. Lightly knead until you have a ball of dough; if it won't come together, add a tiny drop more milk, but not more than half a teaspoon. Flour your surface and roll the dough out to 3mm thick. It's not the easiest dough to work – as you start to roll, it will crack and crumble, but keep clumping it back together between rolls, and as it gets thinner it should get easier to handle. Cut out rounds using your cutter, then bring any off-cuts together and roll the dough out again until you've used it all up. Bake the oatcakes for 15-20 minutes, until crisp and lightly browned. These keep for weeks in an airtight tin.

Drumnadrochit Tomato Ketchup

Makes 3 x 340ml jars

The health benefits of tomato ketchup are well-known. We find some of the commercial varieties too high in sugar and salt, and that Grandma's version is tastier. Ketchup seems to be an essential for Cookie Sunday breakfasts. This ketchup keeps for up to six months in a sealed jar. Ours never lasts that long.

Wash and chop the fresh tomatoes. Put them in a large pot with the tinned tomatoes and slowly bring them up to a simmer. Add the onions, garlic, chilli, ginger, spices and salt. Simmer the mixture gently, stirring frequently, until everything is soft and reduced by a quarter of the original volume. This will take around an hour.

Add the sugar and vinegar to the pot and stir until the sugar dissolves. Leave the ketchup simmering for another hour, stirring regularly. To check if it's done, put a small teaspoonful on a cold plate (as if you were testing jam). It should be thick and all the same consistency; if the sauce separates and clear juice runs out, continue cooking for another 10 minutes and then test it again. When you're happy with the consistency, season the ketchup and blend it with a hand-blender until it's smooth. Decant it immediately into sterilised jars and seal.

1.25kg ripe tomatoes

200g tinned tomatoes

1 large onion, finely chopped

2 garlic cloves, crushed

¼ tsp dried chilli flakes

1cm fresh ginger, grated

1 tsp dried fennel seeds

1 tsp coriander seeds

1 allspice berry, crushed (or use juniper if you prefer)

1 tsp sea salt

85g dark brown sugar

135ml white wine vinegar

freshly ground black pepper

Rhubarb Chutney

Makes 6 x 340ml jars

2 onions, finely chopped

300ml white wine vinegar

5cm fresh ginger, grated

1 tsp ground ginger

150g dried dates, chopped

a pinch of cinnamon

10 cardamom pods, crushed

1kg rhubarb, cut into chunks

400g soft brown sugar

zest and juice of 2
unwaxed oranges

This is a milder chutney than the spicy version in Jacob's section (page 100). It's a great way to use up a glut of rhubarb, and there's nothing like eating your own grown and cooked chutney in the middle of winter to give you a wonderfully smug feeling. It's also very easy.

As usual, sterilise jars either in the dishwasher, by steaming, or by putting them in the oven for 5 minutes at 180°C.

Place the onions, vinegar, fresh and ground ginger, dates and spices into a preserving pan or large pot. Bring the mixture to the boil, and then add the rhubarb, sugar, orange zest and juice. Simmer it gently for about 30 minutes, until the rhubarb is soft but still holding its shape. Put it straight into sterilised jars and seal while still hot.

Rowan and Crab Apple Jelly

Makes about 3 x 340ml jars

1kg rowan berries

1kg crab apples, roughly quartered but cores left in

1.5kg granulated sugar (approximately)

a jelly bag or a muslin

A deciduous tree found throughout Britain, the Rowan is able to grow at higher altitude than any other tree in Scotland. That said, it produces beautiful red berries in autumn at child-friendly height pretty much everywhere. You should pick the berries when they are a full-bodied red colour, but before they turn mushy. Our children have always enjoyed picking them, even though the resulting jelly is more of a cook's staple than a child's choice in a sandwich. Rowan jelly is fabulous with grouse and for adding flavour to gravies and sauces.

Rowan berries were used in the middle ages to scare off evil spirits. You will feel like a witch stirring a cauldron of off-putting ingredients when making this, but it all adds to the mystical ambience. Cook the fruit the night before the jelly is to be made.

Wash the fruit well. Remove all the stalks from the rowan berries and put them in the pan with the quartered crab apples. Pour in enough water to come half way up the fruit, bring it to the boil, and then turn the heat down to a simmer and leave the fruit to cook, stirring from time to time. As it softens, use a large spoon to crush the fruit against the sides of the pan.

When everything is soft and mushy, turn off the heat and tip the lot into your draining material. A jelly bag makes this easy, but what I do is cover the top of a large pan with a muslin, and then tip the mush into it so the pan catches any drips. When all the mush is safely caught, suspend it over the pot and tie it up. We have tried this in many ways: hanging it on the back of a chair or tying it to the knife rack in the kitchen. Basically, you just need to hang it any place where you can leave a large bowl or pot beneath it to catch the juice as it drips through the bag. Leave it overnight.

In the morning, measure the juice in a measuring jug. You can squeeze the bag to get the very last remnants of juice out. This might cause your jelly to be cloudy, but as it's generally used for cooking that doesn't really matter. However, if you want your rowan jelly to be completely clear for a gift or just for perfection, don't touch the bag.

Now comes the maths. For every 500ml of juice you need 375g of sugar. When you've figured out your quantities, put the juice and sugar in your jam pan, heat it slowly until the sugar dissolves, and then bring it to a low rolling boil for 10 minutes. Test a teaspoonful on a cold saucer: if the surface of the jelly wrinkles when you push your finger on one end, it's done. If it doesn't wrinkle, boil it for a further 5 minutes and repeat the test. Leave the jam to cool for a couple of minutes, decant it into sterilised jars, and seal.

Bramble and Apple Jelly

Makes about 3 x 340ml jars

1.5kg brambles, stalks removed

2 large cooking apples, chopped small, pips and core included

juice of 1 lemon

2 kg granulated sugar (approximately: you may need less)

2 tbsp bramble liqueur or cassis (optional)

jelly bag or large muslin

Jellies are absolutely worth the effort: they not only make a brilliant tasting preserve on toast but their culinary uses spread far further. Jellies will brighten up a sponge, make a fantastic glaze, or enrich a gravy. Scotland produces the best brambles around, and the resulting jelly is a unique, vivid purple – it makes a beautiful gift. It's also perfect for brightening up winter, and reminding us of autumn walks.

The cardinal rule is: if you want a beautiful clear jelly, don't squeeze the bag when letting it drain or your jelly will be cloudy.

These quantities are approximate; just use more apples if your bramble pickings are few. The actual quantity of fruit is not really relevant, as the amount of jelly you get will be determined by how much juice drains. You need 450g of sugar for every 600ml of juice, so get a 2kg bag of sugar just to be on the safe side.

Put your washed brambles and apples in a large preserving pan and pour over enough water to come half way up the fruit. Bring it to the boil, stir in the lemon juice and boil for 20 minutes, until the fruit is soft.

Hold your jelly bag or muslin over a large bowl and tip the fruit in, then tie it up and suspend it over the bowl to catch the drips. Leave it overnight.

In the morning, measure your juice. For every 600ml of juice, you will need 450g of sugar, so do the maths and then put the sugar and juice back into your preserving pan. Add the cassis or bramble liqueur (if using) and bring it slowly to the boil. Turn the heat down and simmer the mixture for 10 minutes. Test a teaspoonful on a cold saucer to see if it's reached setting point: if the surface wrinkles when you prod it, it's done. If it's not ready yet, simmer it for another 5 minutes and try again. When it's set, leave it to cool for 2 minutes and then pour into sterilised jars, seal with a wax circle and store.

Marmalade

Makes about 6 x 340ml jars

Grandma makes the best marmalade we've ever tasted. Here is her basic recipe. If you want to make whiskey marmalade, stir in about 4 tablespoons of decent malt just before decanting the marmalade into jars.

Seville oranges are in season in January, and Cookie always stocks them. The recipe can be doubled up easily depending on how many oranges you've got.

Put the oranges into a large pan and cover with boiling water. Leave them overnight, and by the morning they will be soft. Drain them, cut them in half, and squeeze the juice out into a measuring jug. Take out the pips and put them to one side, and then add the lemon juice to the jug. Take note of how much juice you now have, pour it into a large jam pan, and then add enough cold water to make it up to 2 litres. Scrape any remaining flesh out of each squeezed orange half and put it to one side. Cut each orange half into four pieces. Slice these into thin strips and add them to the liquid in the pan. Put the reserved pips and flesh in a muslin bag and tie it onto the saucepan handle with string so it is submerged in the liquid – this will make the next stage much easier.

Bring the mixture up to the boil, and then simmer it on a low heat for about 2 hours. At this point, pull out the muslin bag and leave it on a saucer to cool down. When it's cool enough to handle, squeeze it into the pan to extract all the pectin in the pips, and then discard it. Next, add the sugar and stir until it's dissolved, and then bring it to the boil again. Make sure you have a cold saucer handy. After you've boiled the marmalade for another 15 minutes test it by putting a spoonful on the saucer – prod it and see if it's forming a skin and setting.

If it's ready, stir in a knob of butter and leave the marmalade to cool for 10 minutes before putting it into sterilised jars and sealing. If it isn't set, boil it for 5 more minutes and repeat the test. Don't worry about any froth; the butter will clarify this.

1kg Seville oranges

50ml lemon juice

2kg caster sugar

25g butter

muslin to tie up pips and flesh

Two Raspberry Jams

Raspberries are native to our cooler climes, and Scottish ones are reputedly the best in the world. The best;known varieties are of course red, but in the north of Scotland pale yellow ones grow wild. They are wonderfully versatile fruits for all sorts of tarts and puddings, sorbets and sauces.

All jam recipes follow the same rules, with slight variations for cooking time and for companion flavours. Raspberries are definitely the easiest fruit to make jam with, so if you've never made any before, this is the place to start. A few jars will see you through a winter of jam tarts, Victoria sponges and sandwiches.

900g of raspberries will make 3 x 450g jars.

The Standard Method

raspberries

sugar

Use equal amounts of raspberries and sugar. So, if your children only manage to pick you a couple of handfuls of raspberries, it's still possible to make jam.

Preheat the oven to 180°C.

Sterilise the jars first: you can do this in the dishwasher, or by putting them in the oven for 5 minutes. Pour the sugar into an ovenproof dish and put it in the oven for 10 minutes to warm. Put the raspberries into your jam pan and heat them slowly until the juice starts to run. Carefully tip in the warm sugar and stir well. Bring it up to the boil, and then turn the heat down to medium and boil it for 5 minutes. It will be set, but test it anyway to feel professional: use a cold saucer, put a teaspoonful of the jam on it and push gently. If the surface wrinkles, it's done. Put the jam in your sterilised jars and seal immediately.

Instant Jam (great for small quantities and no mess)

Just to re-emphasize how easy raspberry jam is: you can make it in the oven. The raspberries need to be dry, so if you want to wash them after picking, give them plenty of time to dry properly before starting.

Heat the oven to 200°C. Put the raspberries in an ovenproof dish and an equal weight of caster sugar in another. Bake both for 30 minutes, and then combine them, carefully (they will be hot!), in a heatproof bowl. The raspberries instantly melt with the sugar and become jam. Pot the jam and seal.

Sloe Gin

Makes about a litre

450g sloe berries

350g granulated sugar

1l gin

1.5l airtight storage jar

Prunus spinosa, or blackthorn, does well in the Scottish Highlands. Tradition is to pick the sloe berries in November, a bit like our olives, though ideally they should be picked after the first frost. Watch out for the spikes.

Our usual winter trip is to Alto Adige to ski. This is an area of fantastic beauty on the Italian/Austrian alpine border. The region's 15 minutes of fame came in 1991, when a fully clothed, 5300 year old mummy was discovered. Nicknamed Otzi, the mummy was studied intently as he wore clothes that historians had not believed existed at that time. The main contents of his stomach were sloe berries. I'm fairly sure he didn't make the liqueur, but here is something good to do with berries that have been around since then. This is one my dad makes regularly.

First sterilise your storage jar. Prick each sloe berry (yes each one!) with a clean needle. This takes time – company or the radio helps. Put the pricked sloes into the jar and cover them with the sugar. Pour on the gin, seal the jar and place it in a dark cupboard. Shake it every week or so. It's ready when the gin has turned a deep, reddish purple and all the sugar has dissolved (around 8-10 weeks). Strain the gin into a sterilised bottle and enjoy.

Oscar and Beatrice

Oscar and Beatrice are, at 10 and 5, our youngest children. Cookie makes very few concessions to children: we offer them the same menu as the adults, in smaller portions if required. We take a similar approach at home – our kids eat what we are eating.

Those of us cooking for or around children have less time and often less focus. Yet this is the most important time of our children's lives to develop their taste, understanding and enjoyment. Good eating habits will last a lifetime and help them avoid all those additives and trans-fats in ready-made food.

Children enjoy cooking or helping out in the kitchen. It might mean a bit more work for you, but any hassle really is outweighed by the long-term benefit: if it is normal in your family that food is made from scratch, that cooking is a messy business and one everyone can be involved in, then hopefully you are laying great foundations for their future. And it can be fun.

So this chapter has recipes that children can enjoy – though there are lots more throughout the book. Our kids also really like making pasta, gnocchi, and pizza.

Here you'll find the simple meals that are quick to make, often an essential for family life. And, if I am honest, these are some of my favourites even without the kids.

Fish Fingers

Serves 4

100g breadcrumbs

1 tsp sea salt

zest of 1 lemon

1 tsp turmeric (optional)

1 tsp fresh herbs, finely chopped (optional)

1 free range egg, lightly beaten

450g sustainable white fish (ask your fishmonger what he has that's suitable)

No, not the frozen pieces of poor quality, unsustainable white fish in additive and colour-laden crumbs! These fish fingers are quick to cook, simply prepped and fresh.

In our house, the small kids get these and the adults steal them while waiting for their meal. With great chips, garlic dip and lemon, this can easily be a fantastic adult dinner. I've experimented over the years with various herbs – oregano is lovely, but just add your own choice to the breadcrumbs. Our kids also like a teaspoon of turmeric in the breadcrumbs. This addition originated from a request that I make fish fingers that looked "more like the real thing" (i.e. the frozen packet kind). Turmeric did the job. We use our own leftover bread to make the breadcrumbs – I just use a hand blender and quickly whizz some dry slices.

Preheat the oven to 190°C. In a large bowl, mix the breadcrumbs, salt, lemon zest and the turmeric and any herbs you are using. Put the egg in another bowl.

Cut the fish into even strips – you should get around 14 from this quantity. Grease a baking tray and then get your small, clean-handed helper to dip the strips in egg and then the crumbs, making sure each one is fully covered. By the time the average 4 year old has done all the pieces and placed them on the tray, the oven will be hot.

Bake for about 15 minutes, until golden brown.

Polpetti

Serves 4

At home Nonno makes these and everyone loves them. Cooking meat may not be older children's favourite, but these polpetti are simple, and it's important to get an idea of how to use meat.

Make sure all hands are very clean!

Preheat the oven to 180°C.

In a large bowl combine the meats, chopped onion, nutmeg, salt and pepper. Mix well with your hands, and then add the breadcrumbs, the parsley, the Parmesan and the egg and mix again. You want everything evenly combined. Dust your hands with a bit of plain flour, and roll pieces of the mixture between your palms into balls the size of golf balls – you should end up with about 24. Arrange them in a large casserole, not touching each other too much, and pour over the tomato sauce. Bake for 35 minutes, covered, and then stir gently to combine the sauce and the meat juices. Serve with pasta or mashed potatoes.

250g minced pork

250g minced beef

¼ onion, very finely chopped

a pinch of nutmeg

30g breadcrumbs

10g flat-leaf parsley, finely chopped

25g Parmesan, grated

1 free range egg

1 batch fresh tomato sauce (see page 79)

sea salt

freshly ground black pepper

plain flour for dusting hands

Chicken Milanese

Serves 4

2 tbsp olive oil

½ an onion, very finely chopped

1 garlic clove

400g tin plum tomatoes (or 5 large, peeled plum tomatoes), chopped

2 tbsp flat-leaf parsley

4 free range chicken breasts

100g breadcrumbs

2 free-range eggs, lightly beaten

sea salt

freshly ground black pepper

This recipe is a great one for children to make themselves, and it is healthier for being oven-baked rather than fried. If you're using tinned tomatoes, try and find 'SA' or 'NO' stamped ones from the south of Italy. Breadcrumbs are easy – just put the equivalent amount of stale bread in a food processor and blitz until you have crumbs.

Preheat the oven to 180°C.

First, make the sauce. Heat the olive oil gently and add the onion and garlic. Cook really gently until they're soft, then stir in the tomatoes and simmer until the sauce is just beginning to thicken to a jammy consistency (about 10 minutes). Add the parsley and cook for a further 2 minutes.

While the sauce is simmering, place the chicken breasts between two layers of cling film and beat them with a rolling pin until they are about 2cm thick. Put the breadcrumbs in one bowl, and the eggs, seasoned with salt and pepper, in another. Dip the chicken breasts into the egg and then into the breadcrumbs, making sure that they are evenly covered. Put the chicken on a baking tray and bake for 12 minutes, or until golden.

This goes really well with some cooked spinach.

Parmigana

Serves 8

I've included this recipe in the children's section as it's something they enjoy and can help assemble. This is a great vegetarian dish and a regular Cookie favourite.

This recipe makes enough for eight, but the left-overs are just as good, if not better, eaten cold the next day, so I always make a large one. It's easy enough to halve the recipe if you want to. For the full recipe, you will need a large lasagne dish – mine is 25 x 33cm.

Salting the aubergines draws out any bitterness and improves the texture. Traditionally, aubergines were often grown in rotation with tobacco – both members of the nightshade family of plants – which exaggerated their bitter flavour. However, the bitterness has been largely bred out of the ones you'll find in the shops.

Cut the aubergines into slices about 1cm thick and place them in a colander, sprinkled liberally with a generous amount of salt. Leave them for 30 minutes, then carefully rinse each slice under the cold tap, and squeeze them all gently to get rid of excess water.

Heat the oven to 200°C. Put 4 tablespoons of the oil into a large frying pan over a medium flame and allow it to heat up. Meanwhile, break the eggs into a wide, shallow bowl, and mix in the milk with a fork. Put the flour in another bowl. Dip each slice of aubergine into the eggs, then into the flour, and then fry them in batches so they are nicely browned on each side (this takes about 3 minutes a slice when the oil is good and hot). Add more olive oil as and when you need to, though you may not need the full 200ml. Drain the aubergine on kitchen paper and leave to cool.

These aubergine slices are a meal in themselves: try them as a sandwich, with a slice of fresh tomato and a piece of basil in the middle, drizzled with olive oil. But for the parmigana, you need to arrange the aubergine slices in a dish

4 good-sized aubergines (about 1kg in weight)

200ml olive oil

3 free range eggs

2 tbsp milk

200g plain flour

1 batch tomato sauce (see page 79)

150g Parmesan, finely grated

400g mozzarella, torn into pieces

sea salt

freshly ground black pepper

25 x 33cm lasagne dish

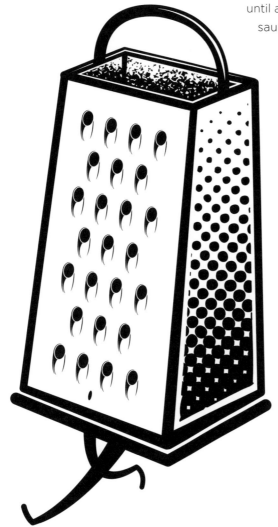

and bake them. Grease the dish lightly, and then build up as follows: start with a layer of aubergines, then a scant spreading of tomato sauce, and then sprinkle on some Parmesan. Season each layer lightly. Repeat until all the aubergines are used up, then pour over any extra sauce, and finish with the mozzarella. You might not feel like you have enough sauce, but stick with it – the end result you're looking for is juicy but compact and not liquid at all. Bake for about 25 minutes, and let it cool a little before serving.

Think lasagne, only better!

Fresh Tomato Sauce

Serves 4-6

It's difficult to know which of the properties of tomatoes to rate the highest: their high vitamin content, with A, B, C, E and K vitamins all in one fruit; or the presence of essential amino acids such as lycene and the antioxidant lycopene, which scientists think may be one of the reasons why there is an inverse relationship between cancer and tomato consumption; or the fact that they are easily available and incredibly useful in the kitchen.

If you are using tinned tomatoes, look for those stamped from Bruno's region of the south of Italy: 'SA' for Salerno and 'NO' for Nocera Inferiore-Gragnano (the famous home of pasta and plum tomatoes).

Choose mature tomatoes, preferably the San Marzano variety.

If you're using fresh tomatoes, boil a large pan of water and drop the tomatoes in until the skins split – 30 to 60 seconds should do it. Drain the tomatoes, and the skins will peel off easily. Cut them in half, remove the hard green area of the stock (I don't bother seeding them), and then chop them roughly.

Heat the oil in a large pan and then fry the garlic gently until it's soft but not brown. Add the tomatoes and simmer for 10 minutes, then add in the basil leaves and simmer for another 5 minutes until the tomatoes have broken down and you have a slightly jammy consistency.

1kg ripe plum tomatoes (or 2 x 400g tins)
125ml olive oil (60ml if using tinned tomatoes)
10 basil leaves, torn
2 garlic cloves, thinly sliced
sea salt

Pesto

The word 'pesto' in Italian simply means crushed, and it comes in many more varieties than the widely known basil pesto. Children love its simplicity and freshness, and as a working mother I love any dinner that is ready as soon as the pasta is done. Here are two of our favourite pestos – make plenty, as it keeps if covered in a layer of olive oil.

Walnut Pesto

Serves 6-8

180g walnuts

100g Parmesan, grated

1 garlic clove

60ml good olive oil

250g ricotta (only use if you're eating the pesto immediately)

With their wonderful, almost meaty flavour, walnuts are my favourite nut. I truly think they go well with everything. We have some really productive trees in Italy, and if Domenico hasn't stripped them to make his walnut liqueur, then I get the kids to collect them all.

In a food processor, grind the walnuts, Parmesan and garlic to a paste. Add the olive oil and put the mixture into a jar, with a thin layer of oil over the top if you're keeping the pesto for later.

If you're eating it there and then, mix the ricotta into the pesto until it's evenly distributed. This is great with gnocchi, or stirred into a plain risotto.

Classic Basil Pesto

Serves 4-6

The quantity of basil given seems huge, I know, and it gets expensive if you are buying it from the supermarket. But the thing about basil is it's incredibly easy to grow: just give it lots of water and, in Scotland, keep it under glass. One of those small pots from the supermarket will double or treble in size in a matter of weeks if you give it a bit of care, and they do very well on a windowsill (near the sink works for me as then I remember to water them daily). Failing that, you could either befriend an allotment gardener, or buy from a wholesale or Chinese market which is significantly cheaper. And if you're still stuck, just use less basil – our editor made it with a 30g bag from the supermarket and it was still delicious.

Traditionally, a pestle and mortar is used to crush the basil, but I use a food processor and it works just fine. This pesto is great on chicken or in a sandwich if you have any left over.

2 tbsp pine nuts

300g basil leaves

25g Parmesan, grated

25g Pecorino, grated

35ml good quality olive oil (approximately)

Lightly toast the pine nuts in a dry pan. Be careful not to burn them: just put them over a low heat until they are a little golden. Put the pine nuts in a pestle and mortar with the basil and pound to a paste, or whizz it all in the food processor.

Stir in the grated cheeses and the oil, mix well and put the pesto in a jar. Pour a little olive oil on the top and store it in the fridge.

Fresh Egg Pasta

Serves 4

1 ½ cups '00' flour plus more for kneading/dusting

¼ cup semolina flour

1 tsp salt

1 free range egg

1 tsp olive oil

Pasta is easy to make. Sure, you don't need to make it, but it can be fun, it makes a special meal and in our house and it is a child-friendly activity. It's a good meal for entertaining as, once you've made the pasta, it's easy to put together just before you eat and doesn't need much to make a really great meal – just some fresh truffle, say, or a simple sauce. We use cups to measure this out.

Mix the flours together, add the salt and make it all into a pile on a clean, flat surface. We make the flour in the shape of a volcano, with a well in the middle. Lightly mix the egg with a fork, stir in the oil, and pour it into the well. Using your fingers, gradually mix the liquid into the flour volcano, letting the flour fall in from the sides. You should end up with a ball of soft dough. Knead the dough on a floured surface until it is even, elastic and not at all sticky, adding a bit more flour if you need to (this will take about 10 minutes). Wrap the dough in cling film and leave it to rest at room temperature for 30 minutes.

You are now ready to make the pasta! If you don't have a pasta maker, no problem – just roll the dough as thinly as you can on a well-floured surface. If you have a machine, take the dough, lightly flour it and roll it through on the widest setting. Click the machine down a setting, push the sheet of dough through again, and continue to work your way through the settings on the machine so you're rolling the sheet thinner and thinner (lightly dust the dough with flour each time to stop it sticking).

Once the sheet is thin and feels silky, cut it into narrow strips (up to 1cm is fine). Lightly flour the strips and leave them spread out and uncovered until you are ready to eat. Fresh pasta only takes 1-2 minutes to cook in a large pan of fiercely boiling, salted water, so get whatever sauce you're having finished first.

Cookie has a range of pasta-making equipment which our chefs will happily lend you if you are nearby. Our family favourite is the pasta 'guitar', which makes thin pieces by pushing the pasta over the strings. Lots of fun!

Pavlova

Serves 6-8

Although meringues are often thought to be tricky, pavlova is actually quite forgiving and works well for children. Any slight imperfections or peculiar shapes are hidden under a pile of cream and fruit, and seriously deformed or broken ones can be broken up, added to strawberries and fresh cream and renamed Eton Mess (see the next recipe). You can use any fruit: strawberries and raspberries are obvious summer options, and in winter we use sliced ripe sharon fruit or pomegranate with the pith removed and the ruby coloured seeds scattered over. Use whatever you have or think looks good.

One of Cookie's favourite customers, Erin, is gluten intolerant. Meringues and pavlova make the perfect sweet alternative for her.

3 free range eggs
175g caster sugar
300ml double
(or whipping) cream
300g fruit
1 tbsp icing sugar

Pre-heat the oven to 150°C, and grease and line a large baking tray with baking paper. Draw a circle about 20°Cm in diameter onto the paper.

Separate the eggs as follows: tap one on the side of a bowl and when you get a crack, gently pull the eggshell into two halves over your bowl, catching the yolk in one half. Tip the yolk from one half of the shell to the other, back and forth, letting all the egg white drop into the bowl. The only really important thing to remember with meringue is that your bowl must be scrupulously clean, and your eggs mustn't have even a speck of egg yolk in them or they will never whisk up, no matter how hard you try. So go carefully.

Using an electric whisk, whisk the egg whites until they make soft peaks, and then add the sugar a spoonful at a time, whisking with each addition. Keep going until all the sugar is in and the meringue forms firm, glossy waves. Get your lined baking tray,

and fill the circle with dollops of the mixture. You can make peaks with a fork if you feel artistic. Put the tray in the oven and immediately turn the heat down to 140°C. Bake it for about an hour, making sure the edges don't burn. If you can, turn the oven off and leave the pavlova in overnight with the door slightly ajar. If you haven't got time, just leave it to cool on a wire rack.

Just before serving, whip the cream until it's thick, and spread it lightly in the centre of the meringue. Scatter over the fruit and lightly dust with a tablespoon of icing sugar through a sieve. It's easy and delicious.

Eton Mess

Serves 6-8

1 pavlova (see page 83)

450g strawberries, hulled

1 tbsp icing sugar

500ml double cream

For this you need a pavlova, as per the previous recipe, but it should be broken up - so perhaps it's the one your child leant on, or the one that didn't quite rise perfectly. If it's winter and you don't have strawberries, you can make this with more seasonal fruit. I guess it's not called Eton mess then, as that name came from the tradition of strawberries and cream served in a very English way at a very English school. But any fruit saves the duff pavlova from being wasted.

Smash the pavlova into pieces, but don't grind it to a powder. In a bowl, blend half the strawberries to a pulp and stir in the icing sugar. Chop the rest of the strawberries into quarters, and keep a handful aside. Whip the cream until it is just beginning to thicken, and then fold in the smashed meringue and the quartered fruit. Gently mix through most of the fruit puree to give a marbled look. Serve this in a large bowl, topped with the reserved puree and fruit, or in individual ice cream glasses.

Jam Tarts

Makes around 16

Following on from a local community jam-making event, Cookie had a huge excess of jam, so the children made these tarts at their cooking class. Very retro. Very simple. And a good chance to learn how to make pastry.

Sift the flour and sugar into a large bowl. Cut the cold butter into small cubes and rub it into the flour with your fingertips, gently, until it is like breadcrumbs. Then gradually add the cold water, a little at a time, and mix it all gently until you have one lump of dough that binds together (you may not need all the water). Wrap the dough in cling film and put it in the fridge for 30 minutes.

Heat the oven to 180°C. Take the pastry out of the fridge, and leave it for a minute while you flour a flat surface and a rolling pin. Roll the pastry to 5mm thick. Grease your tart tin and, with a cutter or a cup, cut out a circle just big enough to cover each holder in the tin. Press in the pastry gently, and fill the centre with a teaspoonful of jam or curd. Don't over fill, about half full is perfect as it will spread out in the oven.

Any left over pastry can be squashed together and rolled out again. We cut out pastry stars with a small cutter and put these on top of the jam tarts.

Bake in the oven for about 12 minutes. Cool on a wire rack before eating.

200g '00' or plain flour
½ tsp caster sugar
100g fridge-cold unsalted butter
2-3 tbsp ice cold water
jam or lemon curd (see the next recipe)

tin for the tarts

Lemon or Lime Curd

Makes 2 x 250ml jars

4 unwaxed lemons

100g unsalted butter

3 free range eggs

1 free range egg yolk

200g sugar

Lemon curd is really easy. It makes a great filling for Victoria sponges or jam tarts and keeps well in the fridge for a couple of weeks. This makes enough to fill two jars, so have them sterilised and ready.

Grate the zest from the lemons and squeeze the juice into a jug. Cut the butter into small cubes, and mix the eggs and extra yolk lightly with a fork in a bowl.

Heat a small pan of water to boiling, turn it down to a simmer and place a heatproof bowl over the top of the pan so it doesn't touch the water. Put the sugar, lemon juice, zest and butter into the bowl and keep stirring with a wooden spoon until the butter has melted. Then add the eggs and stir some more. This part takes about 8 minutes – you need to keep stirring as the mixture thickens to stop it scrambling, but soon enough it will coat the back of the spoon and become thick and smooth. Take it off the heat and pot into jars.

Victoria Sponge

Serves 8-10

The enduring popularity with children of a Victoria sponge always amazes me. Although, thinking it through, it's not far off of a large jam sandwich. It's really easy to make but makes a fantastic centrepiece, and it always gives our young cooks a real sense of satisfaction. As a child, Domenico's failed sponges were reconstituted by Bruno into the base for trifle, with the addition of a bit of alcohol.

The recipe doubles up easily and can be made in pretty much any shape. The cooking times here are for two cakes made in 21cm round tins – if the cake batter is spread thinner, it will take less time; if it's thicker, it will take longer. Check with a skewer poked in the middle of the cake, which will come out crumb-free when it's done.

Preheat the oven to 180°C. Grease and line your tins with greaseproof paper.

In a large bowl, cream the butter and sugar together until it's pale and fluffy, almost like a mousse. Add the vanilla, and then beat in two of the eggs and a tablespoon of flour (an electric whisk makes the shortest work of this). When fully combined, beat in the remaining eggs and a further tablespoon of flour, and then fold in the rest of the flour and the baking powder. Finally, add the milk and mix gently until you have a soft, dropping consistency.

Spread the batter evenly into the tins and bake for about 25 minutes, until the cakes are golden and pulling away from the sides of the tins. Try not to open the oven until the time is up.

Carefully remove the cakes from their tins and cool on a wire rack. When they're cool, put one of the cakes on your serving plate and spread with jam. Put the fruit in a single layer on top, and then whip the cream to soft folds and spoon over the fruit. Gently press the second cake on top and dust it with icing sugar through a sieve.

225g unsalted butter

225g caster sugar

1 tsp vanilla extract (or the scraped insides of a $\frac{1}{2}$ of a vanilla pod)

4 free range eggs

230g self-raising flour

$\frac{1}{2}$ tsp baking powder

2 tbsp milk

4 tbsp jam

a punnet of raspberries or strawberries, depending on preference

125ml double cream

2 tbsp icing sugar

2 x 21cm cake tins

Banana Bread

Serves 8-10

150g soft brown sugar

125g unsalted butter, melted

2 free range eggs, lightly beaten

350g really over-ripe bananas (about 3 whole bananas)

½ tsp vanilla extract

80g nuts (optional)

150g dried fruit (optional)

50g chocolate chips (optional)

180g plain flour

½ tsp bicarbonate of soda

2 tsp baking powder

¼ tsp cinnamon

¼ tsp nutmeg

23 x 13 x 7cm loaf tin

This is one of the easiest cakes in the world. As I'm writing this, our 5 year old is 'making' one all by herself: the kitchen looks a bit like a war zone, but the end result will taste great. It tastes best when made with those really past it, over-ripe black bananas, and it's fantastic for packed lunches as it holds its shape when cut.

This recipe does not really demand anything other than the butter, flour, raising agents and sugar (plain caster sugar is fine if that's what you have). I add chocolate chips if I happen to have any and am feeling kind and generous. Chopped dates are good, but any dried fruit like raisins will do. Nuts, again, are only if you want them. I keep a vanilla pod in a jar of sugar, because it's easy and it means I don't need to add vanilla extract when I'm baking. If you're not in the habit of doing so, use the vanilla extract or scrape the inside of half a vanilla pod into the batter.

Heat the oven to 160°C. Grease and line your loaf tin with greaseproof paper. In a large bowl, whisk together the sugar, melted butter and eggs. Mash the bananas and add them, and then beat in the vanilla extract and any or all of the optional nuts, dried fruit or chocolate chips.

In another bowl, sift together the flour, bicarbonate of soda, baking powder, cinnamon and nutmeg. Fold the dry ingredients into the wet banana mixture until it's well combined. Pour the batter into the tin and bake for about an hour. It's ready when a skewer comes out clean.

Soda Bread

Bread is a really good learning skill for children as it's so much easier than anyone imagines. Our daughter's Steiner kindergarten bakes bread every week, and it's really lovely to see all the children participating. I've done soda bread here as it's so quick – a great afternoon project, with relatively instant results.

We use Ed's Honey because it's local, but any runny honey will do. This recipe will bear some experimenting: you can add 80g of any seeds you fancy, and the flour can be changed to plain white or rye or really any speciality flour you like – just keep the quantities the same.

250g wholemeal flour
80g seeds (optional)
1 tsp bicarbonate of soda
100ml whole milk
100ml plain yoghurt
2 tbsp runny honey
1 tbsp olive oil

Heat the oven to 200°C. Grease a baking tray and shake some flour on top.

Mix the flour, seeds (if you're using them), and bicarbonate of soda in a bowl. In a measuring jug, stir the milk, yoghurt, honey and oil together. Make a well in the middle of the flour and pour the liquid into it. Mix it with your hands, or get your messy helper to do this. When it is in one sticky lump, dump it onto the baking tray; appearance at this point is not important. Cut a cross on the top, about 1cm deep, and bake for 25 minutes until it's golden brown. Cool the bread on a wire rack.

This bread is recommended for late afternoon TV watching with plenty of jam and butter.

Jacob

Smugness has never been a Cookie trait, either in the business or at home; we are far too firmly grounded in reality. One of life's realities is that no matter how much freshly cooked, healthy food you give people, there are those who will always prefer McDonald's.

All our children have been brought up in and around food. In Italy, it's expected that they learn to appreciate the animals, the land, and fresh seasonal vegetables. Jacob though – he prefers junk food. While the other three are happy with spinach, he eats it on sufferance. It may be age, it may be a phase, but this part of the book is dedicated to Cookie's attempts to do really tasty, easy to eat food: dishes that are home-cooked but recognisable to contemporary culture and combine a balance of fresh ingredients done well.

No trans-fats, but plenty of zing. These are the dishes Jacob will order when he is in Cookie. With no side of salad.

Frittura

Serves 4–6

500g '00' flour

1 tbsp baking powder

1 tsp olive oil

400ml cold water, ideally sparkling mineral water (approximately)

a pinch of salt

vegetable oil for deep frying

sea salt and wedges of lemon to serve.

Also:

500g fish and shellfish:

- squid, prepared and cut into rings
- small sprats or any fish small and suitable to fry whole
- whole raw peeled prawns
- large chunks of any white fish fillet that's thick enough to hold its shape.

Mixed vegetables of your choice. We particularly like:

- fresh sage leaves
- small chunks of courgette
- broccoli cut into florets
- sliced red peppers

One of our favourite festivals in the summer is in a tiny village called Montoro that specialises in frittura. Frittura translates, basically, as 'fried things', though fried in a light batter. Fresh fish is fantastic done like this, as are most vegetables. We usually make the quantity of batter specified, and then use it for whatever fish we've bought – any left over batter gets used with whatever vegetables we happen to have. If you need more batter, it's very quick to whisk up another bowl.

You will need a big pan of oil (enough for deep frying), a metal slotted spoon to remove the cooked frittura and kitchen paper to drain.

If you are doing a large quantity, keep each batch warm in an oven heated to about 140°C until you've finished frying the lot.

Make the batter. Sift the flour into a large bowl (I use a food processor). Add the baking powder, and then stir in the oil. Slowly pour in the water, whisking (or whizzing in a food processor) all the time. Keep adding water until you have a smooth, lump-free batter. It should be thick enough to coat the back of a spoon but still easy to pour. Add the pinch of salt last, and give it a final whisk.

Heat the oil while you prepare your veg and fish into small chunks.

When the oil is hot enough to quickly cook a small piece of bread, you can start to fry. Dip individual pieces of veg and fish into the batter, and then immediately slide them into the hot oil – you can do a few in the pan at once. They will be ready in about a minute, as soon as they turn golden brown and crisp. (Sage leaves cook in a few seconds). Remove the frittura and drain on kitchen paper. Serve them with some salt and wedges of lemon to squeeze.

Chicken Liver Pâté

Serves 6

This is a really easy, economical pâté to make. It goes well with our oatcakes (see page 62), some chutney and a glass of wine.

Cut off 100g of the butter, divide it in half and set it aside. Melt one of the 50g pieces gently in a frying pan, taking care not to burn it. Add the garlic, thyme and the chicken livers and fry them gently for 5 minutes, turning all the time. Season them with salt and pepper. Remove the livers with a slotted spoon and put them in the blender, but leave the juices in the pan. In a small saucepan or the microwave, melt the largest remaining chunk of butter (125g).

Pour the brandy onto the juices left in the pan, and add the liquid to the blender, scraping in any bits left behind. Pour in the melted butter and blend the mixture to a smooth paste, then pot it into either small individual ramekins or one large dish. Melt the final piece of butter (50g), and pour a small amount over the top of each pot to seal. Refrigerate.

225g butter
1 garlic clove, crushed
2 sprigs of thyme (leaves only), finely chopped
225g chicken livers
1 tbsp brandy
sea salt
freshly ground black pepper

Suppli

Makes about 15

2 tbsp butter

300g arborio rice
(or left-over risotto)

600ml vegetable stock
(approximately)

1 tbsp tomato puree

80g Parmesan, grated

250g mozzarella, cut into
1cm cubes

1 free range egg,
lightly beaten

180g breadcrumbs

oil for frying

These are a big family favourite. They originated as a way of using up left over risotto, but you can make them with freshly cooked arborio rice too, and they make a fantastic appetiser.

Cook the rice, risotto style, as follows. Melt the butter, add the rice and stir to coat it with the melted butter. Then add the stock, a ladleful at a time, stirring all the while until the stock is absorbed. Continue this way until the rice is cooked (about 20 minutes).

Once the rice is *al dente*, stir in the tomato puree and grated Parmesan, and then leave the mixture to cool. When it's cool, get a tablespoonful of the rice and form it into an oval ball. Then, using your thumb, make an indentation in the middle and poke a couple of mozzarella cubes into it. Reform the rice firmly over the top, pinching with your fingers and then rolling it in your hands to smooth the surface. You need to make sure the rice completely covers the mozzarella. Repeat the process until you've used up all the rice (you should get about 15 of them).

Put the egg and the breadcrumbs in two shallow bowls.. Pour oil into a frying pan to about 5cm deep, and put the pan over a medium heat to get good and hot. Meanwhile, coat each rice ball in the beaten egg and then roll them thoroughly in the breadcrumbs. Fry them in batches in the hot oil until they're golden brown all over, turning them as and when you need to. Drain them on kitchen paper and eat immediately.

Stuffed Zucchini

Serves 4

As a teenager, Domenico spent a summer in the north of Italy working for the well-known silversmith Lino Sabatini. Lino lived in a house not unlike the one in Jacques Tati's Mon Oncle. It was an austere household, but his sister Adriana was a great cook and, surprised that a boy was interested in cooking, she took Domenico to her heart and showed off many of her recipes and cooking techniques. This recipe comes from her and we often use it at Cookie as a starter or part of the antipasti platter. It is a good place for a beginner or student to start and is great on a budget.

This recipe is included here as, although Jacob would never request simple courgettes, he really enjoys these – probably due to the fact that they are really tasty, and the actual vegetable is not visibly a courgette but serves as a small plate.

Cut the courgettes in half lengthwise, and then use a spoon to carve out the middle all the way along the length to make a canoe. Finely chop the scrapings, sprinkle them with salt and leave them in a colander to drain for 30 minutes. This draws out the water and reduces the volume a bit.

Set the oven to 180°C. Rinse the salt from the chopped courgette scrapings and mix them with the minced pork, Parmesan, breadcrumbs and lemon zest. Stir in the basil, and then add the eggs to bind the stuffing together.

Pack your zucchini canoes with the stuffing, put them snugly in a roasting tray and pour over the stock and the wine. Drizzle the canoes with olive oil, season them, and pop the tray in the oven for 30 minutes.

4 courgettes

150g lean pork mince

150g Parmesan

60g breadcrumbs

zest of 1 unwaxed lemon

a good handful of fresh basil, roughly chopped

2 free range eggs, lightly beaten

280ml chicken or vegetable stock

60ml white wine

olive oil

sea salt

freshly ground black pepper

Pizza for Jacob

Makes 8

325ml lukewarm water

1 tsp sugar

½ tbsp dried yeast (or 15g fresh)

500g '00' or plain flour

½ tbsp cooking salt

2 tbsp olive oil, plus extra for drizzling

toppings of your choice (see our ideas below)

Start with activating the yeast. Put 100ml of the tepid water into a small jug and add the sugar and the yeast. Leave for 10 minutes, by which point you should have a frothy head, like on a German beer.

Put the flour in a large mixing bowl and add the salt. Make a well in the middle and pour in the olive oil, the foaming yeasty water and the remaining 225ml of water. Mix it with your hands (or with the dough hook on your mixer) until the dough comes together in one ball. Then turn the dough out onto a floured work surface and knead for 10 minutes by hand (or 5 minutes in your mixer), until it's smooth and elastic. Lightly grease a clean bowl with olive oil, put in the dough the bowl, then cover it with cling film and leave it in a warm place to double in size (around an hour in Scotland).

Once the dough has risen, knock the air out of it by giving it a big punch and repeat the kneading process for 5 minutes by hand (or 2 minutes in your mixer). Divide the dough in half, half it again, and then half it again until you get eight clementine-sized balls. Roll each piece into a ball with your hands, sprinkle them with flour and cover them with a clean dish towel. At this point, they are freezable and you have done most of the work. (If you want to freeze the dough, flour each ball well, put them in individual freezer bags, and then place them straight into the freezer. When you need them, just defrost and let the dough come to room temperature, and you're ready to roll out your pizzas).

All you need now is a very hot oven (240°C is good) and a range of toppings. As a family, we get everyone to do their own. Prepare a clean, floured flat surface. Take a ball of dough and, with a good rolling pin, roll it out as flat as you can. You can tell pizza in Rome from pizza in Naples by the thickness of the dough: the Romans like it wafer thin. We usually aim for somewhere between the two. When the pizza is flat, put on your toppings (see below for our ideas). Just before it goes in the oven, drizzle it with olive oil, and add a pinch of sea salt. Slide your pizza onto a baking tray and put it in the hot oven. The pizzas are ready when the edges of the dough are golden brown and the toppings are bubbling (about 8-10 minutes).

Toppings

For the tomato base, simply drain a tin of plum tomatoes and smash them with a wooden spoon or potato masher to make a slightly thicker, saucier consistency. Add a half teaspoon of salt. Smear the sauce thinly onto the pizza and add:

- fresh mozzarella

- anchovy and mozzarella

- thinly sliced potato (parboil for 6 minutes and drain) with chopped rosemary, salt and garlic

- zucchini flowers and anchovy

- pan-fried sausage, mushroom and garlic

- anchovy and capers

- slices of pear and gorgonzola cheese

The possibilities are endless and the rules your own. We always finish with a chocolate spread pizza – cook a plain pizza with just olive oil, and spread on the chocolate when the pizza comes out of the oven and is still hot. A slightly more adult version of this pizza is chocolate spread with fresh ricotta.

Cookie Burger, Jacob-style

Serves 4

*2 extra thick slices of
stale bread*

1 onion, roughly chopped

*1 celery stalk, roughly
chopped*

1 handful flat-leaf parsley

1 tbsp tomato puree

500g minced beef

*1 free range egg,
lightly beaten*

sea salt

freshly ground black pepper

Cookie's Jacob-style burger was inspired by our neighbour. We live in Scotland's largest Asian area, surrounded by some fantastic cooks: our neighbour cooks delicious koftas, and blends the vegetables to get a lovely smooth texture. If you prefer a rougher, more homemade version, simply chop the vegetables instead of blending them.

Firstly, zap the bread into crumbs using a hand-blender or food processor and put them in a large bowl. Next, process the onion, celery, parsley and tomato puree to a runny, smooth-ish consistency. Scrape this into the bowl with the breadcrumbs, then add all the remaining ingredients and mix thoroughly using your hands. You need a mixture that will hold its shape, so if it's too runny, add some more breadcrumbs. Leave to rest for 30 minutes, covered.

Preheat the oven to 180°C and lightly grease a baking tray with olive oil. Then shape the burgers by hand and place them on the tray. You should have enough for about eight burgers from this mixture.

Cook for 30 minutes, turning the burgers after 15, until they're cooked through.

Sweet Chilli Sauce

Makes about 100ml

This is the kind of dip Jacob thinks adds flavour to everything. It's good with anything you like to dip, drizzled over pâté on oatcakes, or on small canapes. You can buy small bottles of this, but your own will be tastier, fresher and slightly stronger.

Put the sugar and water in a small, heavy-based saucepan. Stir to dissolve the sugar over a low heat, and then bring it to a rolling boil for 5-8 minutes, or until it's reduced and thickened and turned a light golden colour..

In the meantime, put the garlic, ginger, red chillies and lime juice in a food processor and whiz it to a coarse paste – if your food processor can't cope with small quantities, just chop it all finely and then mash it in a mortar and pestle.

When the sugar syrup is ready, carefully stir in the chilli paste. Return the mixture to the boil, and simmer it for another couple of minutes. Allow it to cool down completely before serving.

60g caster sugar

4 tbsp water

3 garlic cloves, peeled and roughly chopped

3cm fresh ginger, roughly chopped

2 long red chillies (according to taste), deseeded and roughly chopped

1 large lime, juice only

Apple Chutney

Makes 3 x 340ml jars

800g cooking apples,
peeled and chopped

1 big onion

3 dried red chillies

400g soft brown sugar

3cm piece of fresh ginger,
finely chopped

1 1/2 tsp ground cloves

1 1/2 tsp ground allspice

1 1/2 tbsp turmeric

560ml cider or malt vinegar

sea salt

freshly ground black pepper

There are many variations on chutney, but this one is great with cheese or on a burger. It's surprisingly easy to make: all you need is a big pan. Jars can be sterilised in the dishwasher, by steaming, or by putting them in the oven at 180°C for 5 minutes.

Put everything into a big pan and bring it to a boil. Turn the heat down to medium and simmer the mixture, stirring every so often to avoid it sticking. Continue for 30-40 minutes, until the chutney thickens.

Spoon the chutney into the clean, sterilised jars and leave them to cool before putting on the lids.

Basic White Bread

This really is very simple, and only takes about 2 hours all in. You will need a 900g loaf tin if you are aiming to make a classic sandwich loaf. If not, shape it as you like; remember the dough will double in size.

Activate the yeast by putting 100ml of the water into a small jug and stirring in the sugar and the yeast. Leave it for 15 minutes, by which time a frothy head should develop.

Tip the flour into a big bowl and rub in the butter with your fingertips. Add the salt. Pour in the yeasty water and the remaining 250ml of water, and mix it all with your hands (or in a machine with a dough hook) until it comes together. Turn the dough out onto a floured surface and knead it for 10 minutes (or 5 minutes in a mixer), until it's smooth and elastic. Then leave the dough to prove in a floured bowl, covered with a clean cloth, for up to an hour.

When the dough has doubled in size, punch all the air out (it's therapy), and again turn it out onto a floured surface and knead it for 5 minutes (or 3 in a mixer).

If you're using a tin, grease it with butter; if you're going freeform, grease a baking tray. Put the dough in the tin or shape it into the rough shape you want, smoothing off the top with damp hands. Leave it to double in size again (about 30 minutes).

Meanwhile, preheat your oven to 200°C. (Generally, if your oven is slow to heat and it's cold, you should put it on when you leave the bread to rise for the second time).

With a very sharp knife, make three small slashes on the top of your loaf and dust the top with a small handful of flour. Bake it at 200°C for 10 minutes, and then turn the heat down to 190°C and bake it for a further 20 minutes.

To test for doneness, take the bread out and tap the bottom: it's done if it sounds hollow, so leave it to cool on a rack or balanced somehow so that air gets all around it. If it doesn't sound hollow, put it straight back in the oven, minus the tin, for another 5 minutes.

350ml tepid water

1 tsp sugar

1 tbsp dried yeast (or 30g of fresh)

500g stong bread flour

1 tbsp butter, softened

1 tsp cooking salt (not sea salt)

extra flour for kneading

900g loaf tin

Sticky Toffee Pudding

Serves 8–10

Pudding

200g dried dates, chopped

250ml tea

½ tsp bicarbonate of soda

175g muscovado sugar

85g butter

2 free range eggs

175g self-raising flour

1 tsp mixed spice

Sauce

100g muscovado sugar

100g unsalted butter

150ml single cream

20 x 30cm brownie pan

This is a classic Cookie pudding. We like it at home, as it's even better re-heated. It's simple to make and great with ice cream or custard for extra indulgence.

Preheat the oven to 180°C and butter an ovenproof dish: I use a brownie pan (20 x 30cm) which makes slicing really easy.

Put the dates and tea in a pan and bring it to the boil. Take it off the heat and leave to cool for a few minutes, then add the bicarbonate of soda. With an electric whisk, beat the sugar and butter in a separate bowl until they are pale and fluffy. Whisk in the eggs, one by one, with a tablespoon of flour after each, and then fold in the rest of the flour and the mixed spice. Finally, stir in the soaked dates and mix well. Pour the batter into the tin and bake for 35 minutes, until it's firm to the touch.

About 10 minutes before the pudding is cooked, start on the sauce. Put the sugar, butter and cream in a small pan over a low heat. Once the sugar has dissolved, continue cooking it gently, stirring from time to time, until you have a thick but pourable golden sauce.

Serve the hot pudding and sauce together, with ice cream or custard if you like.

Custard

Serves 4-6

Jacob loves custard – the tinned stuff he can buy in the corner shop. One look at the ingredients, and most of us would make our own. It's just as quick, though not quite as yellow.

In a bowl, whisk the egg yolks, sugar and cornflour together until frothy. In a small pan (a milk pan with a lip for pouring is perfect), bring the milk, cream and vanilla up to a simmer. Pour the hot milk mixture onto the yolks, whisking all the time. When it's all in, pour the contents of the bowl back into the pot, and stir it gently over a low heat until the custard thickens (it should coat the back of a wooden spoon). Our chefs put the pan into an ice bath at this point, and stir the custard until it's cool. At home, competing against the tinned variety which Jacob tells me is quicker and therefore better, I don't bother.

Either eat it hot or, when the custard's cool, rest a piece of cling film on the surface to stop a skin forming.

4 free range egg yolks

30g caster sugar

2 tsp cornflour

570ml whole milk

50ml single cream

1 vanilla pod
(or ½ tsp vanilla extract)

Lemon Pavlova

Serves 8-10

Meringue

4 free range egg whites

a pinch of cream of tartar

225g caster sugar

2 tsp cornflour

1 tsp vinegar

½ tsp vanilla extract (or the scraped insides of a ½ of a vanilla pod)

Filling

4 free range egg yolks

115g caster sugar

3 tbsp lemon juice

zest of an unwaxed lemon, finely grated

295ml double cream

icing sugar to serve

When we first opened Cookie, most of the baking came from me, or our friend Allison Lironi, who kept all her grandmother's recipes secret until she was bullied into sharing them for this book.

Grandma Liz's recipes came compiled, indexed and laminated, retaining her original and very random comments beside them: 'best yet', 'really easy' and my favourite, 'good for scouts' (whatever that meant!).

Her lemon pavlova is now a regular feature at Cookie.

Preheat the oven to 140°C. Line two large baking sheets with greaseproof paper.

With an electric whisk, beat the egg whites and cream of tartar until they hold firm peaks. Add the sugar, a tablespoon at a time, and continue to whisk after each addition. When all the sugar has been added, sprinkle over the cornflour and carefully fold in the vinegar and vanilla with a metal spoon.

Onto each baking tray, spread half the mixture in a circle, roughly the size of a large dinner plate. Bake the trays for 45-60 minutes, until the meringues are tinged with gold and crisp. Leave them to cool on a wire rack.

While the meringues are cooling, get on with the filling. Beat the egg yolks and sugar until creamy, and then add the lemon juice and zest. Transfer the filling into a small saucepan and cook over a gentle heat, stirring constantly, until it thickens enough to coat the back of your wooden spoon. Leave it to cool, and then beat in the double cream. It should be thick enough to spread but still keep its shape.

Carefully peel your cooled meringues off the greaseproof paper and sandwich them together with the creamy lemon curd. Dust the lemon pavlova with icing sugar to serve.

Brownies

Makes 12

As we know, these were never going to be the healthy option. At home they are cut up into much smaller sizes than our Cookie customers would be willing to pay for!

We make many variations on the basic recipe below, depending on what's in the cupboard. Ground almonds, instead of flour, make a great gluten-free alternative version; dates are also a good addition, and you can swap any nuts you like for the walnuts – just add about 100g at the end.

Preheat the oven to 180°C.

Grease and line your tin with greaseproof paper. Melt the butter and chocolate together over a low heat, and then leave it to cool for 5 minutes. Whisk the yolks with the sugar until pale and creamy, and then add the chocolate and butter mixture and whisk some more. Fold in the flour. With clean beaters and a clean bowl, whisk the egg whites until they're firm, and then fold them into the chocolate batter. Finally, fold in the nuts.

Pour the batter into the tin and bake for about 20 minutes. Leave it to cool and cut the brownies into squares while still in the tin. They're fantastic with ice cream.

200g dark chocolate (70% cocoa solids)

200g unsalted butter

4 free range eggs, separated into yolks and whites

250g caster sugar

120g '00' or plain flour (or 200g ground almonds)

100g walnuts, finely chopped (optional)

22cm square brownie tin

Elliott

Elliott is our oldest. As we are writing this book, he's working in Cookie as part of a gap year mostly spent travelling. He's a great waiter, and not too bad in the kitchen either. He leaves home for university later this year. He loves his food and can cook well. Knowing that he'll be on a student budget and is new to cooking for himself, this section of the book is dedicated to Cookie's most basic and inexpensive recipes. It's heavy on the breakfast items, as brunch at Cookie seems to be one of his main meals these days, and he says he'll miss the Stornaway Tower.

These recipes should provide a basis for some good nutritious meals, as well as a few that make good meals for friends. Economical cooking for one is all about dishes that, if you've taken the time to cook them, will do for the next day's lunch or can be rehashed the next evening slightly differently. Food waste should be on everyone's agenda. Italian cooking is firmly rooted in making the most of left-overs, looking at ways to make several meals out of one main item and a general respect for produce, which means you waste nothing.

We think this approach should work for everyone, but it's a great starting point, particularly if you're on a tight budget. Elliott's off to Aberdeen; we really hope he'll make good use of the cheap fish there, visit the markets, and cook for us all when we visit.

Two Good Stocks

For economy, you can't beat soup.
The essential ingredient is good stock.

Each recipe makes about 2 litres

Chicken Stock

I often use a whole chicken and then eat the poached meat cold, but you can just as well use a raw carcass or the remains of a roast.

Put all the ingredients into a large saucepan and cover them with 3 litres of water. Bring it slowly to the boil, and then turn down the heat and simmer, covered, for about 1 ½ hours. Strain the stock over a large bowl, putting aside the chicken if you used a whole one, as it's ready to use. I usually freeze the stock in batches of 500ml to a litre so I always have some handy.

1.5kg free range chicken, all fatty parts removed (or a cooked or raw chicken carcass)

2 carrots, scrubbed

2 sticks celery, cleaned

1 garlic clove

1 small onion, peeled

5 bay leaves

3 sprigs of fresh thyme

1 tsp whole black peppercorns

Vegetable Stock

Put the oil in a large pan over a medium heat and add all of the ingredients. Stir it well, and then cover the pan and sweat the mixture for 5 minutes, taking care not to burn anything. Pour over 3 litres of water and bring it to the boil, and then lower the heat and simmer it all, covered, for an hour. Strain the stock over a bowl and it's ready to go – again, great for freezing in batches.

1 tbsp olive oil

½ onion, roughly chopped

½ leek, roughly chopped

1 carrot, scrubbed

1 fennel bulb, quartered

3 garlic cloves

1 tbsp whole black peppercorns

1 celery stalk, roughly chopped

3 tomatoes, quartered

4 stalks fresh parsley

Butternut Squash Soup with Cumin

Serves 6

1 butternut squash

2 garlic cloves, finely chopped

1 tsp cumin seeds

2 tsp dried chilli flakes

1 tbsp sea salt

4 tbsp olive oil

1 medium onion, finely chopped

1l stock, either chicken or vegetable (see page 108)

freshly ground black pepper

This is a lovely soup – always a favourite in Cookie – and it has a much deeper taste than you might expect. The cumin compliments the sweetness of the squash brilliantly. If you're in a hurry, you can leave out the roasting part of the recipe and, instead, add the squash and spices to the pan with the onion, sweating them with the lid on for 10 minutes before you add the stock. You will, however, need to simmer the soup gently for 35 minutes before blending.

Preheat the oven to 190°C. Peel and chop the squash into cubes, keeping as much flesh as possible. Put the cubes in a bowl with the garlic, cumin seeds, chilli flakes, salt and 3 tablespoons of the olive oil. Mix it well with your hands so everything is well coated, and then place it all in a large roasting tin and put it in the oven for 35-40 minutes, turning the cubes occasionally to prevent any burning. When the squash is soft and tinged with gold, remove it from the oven.

In a large pan on a gentle heat, sweat the onion in the remaining tablespoon of oil until it's translucent. Add the contents of the roasting dish, scraping in all the oil and stray spices. Pour in the stock, give it a stir and bring it to the boil. Simmer the soup for 10 minutes, and let it cool a bit before blending to a smooth consistency. Give it some freshly ground black pepper and serve.

Frances' Chicken Soup

Serves 15 (but freezes well)

This recipe comes from our friend Frances Bernstein, the best of all Jewish mothers, who has been cooking chicken soup every Friday night for forever. She is a great cook with a lot of fantastic recipes, but her chicken soup is a good choice when you are missing a bit of home. She says this recipe could feed a whole army, but you can't really make less. It can be portioned off and then frozen.

The first thing to know is that chicken soup is best made with a boiling hen – ideally a Kosher one. If you can't get one, use a free range chicken.

Clean the chicken and cut it into quarters, leaving the skin on. Clean the vegetables and roughly chop.

Put everything but the chicken into a large soup pot. Pour in enough water to fill your pot three-quarters of the way, and bring it all to the boil. Turn the stock down to a gentle simmer, and then carefully slide in the chicken pieces. Cover the soup and simmer it very slowly – so the surface is just trembling – for 2 ½ hours. Keep checking that it doesn't start to boil.

When the time is up, leave the soup to cool and then skim off the fat that solidifies on the surface. You can keep this for cooking the kniedlach (see recipe below), or discard it. Take out the chicken and shred the flesh, discarding the skin, then return it to the pot.

Season the soup and serve it hot with kniedlach (see page 112).

1.5kg chicken

6 carrots, roughly chopped

2 celery stalks, roughly chopped

1 large onion, roughly chopped

1 leek, roughly chopped

1 parsnip, roughly chopped

1 tsp salt

2 Kosher chicken stock cubes (like Telma or Osem)

1 tsp sugar

Kniedlach

Makes 15-20

2 ½ tbsp margarine (or
chicken fat from the top of
the chicken soup)

3 large free range eggs

1 ¼ cups Rakusen medium
matzo meal (or oats if
unavailable)

1 tsp salt

½ tsp cinnamon

These are Frances's classic dumplings to go with her chicken soup.

Boil a kettle of water. Melt the margarine (or fat) and pour it into a large bowl. Add 3 tablespoons of boiling water and beat in the eggs. In another bowl, mix together the matzo meal, the salt and the cinnamon. Add the dry ingredients to the eggs, spoonful by spoonful, beating well between each one, until everything is mixed together evenly. Leave the dough, covered, in the fridge for at least an hour.

Bring a large pan of lightly salted water to the boil. With wet hands, make small, walnut-sized balls of dough, drop them into the boiling water, and then simmer, half covered, for 40 minutes. Leave the dumplings in a colander to drain and dry off a bit, and then put them in the hot soup when you're ready to serve it.

Cacio e Pepe

Serves 4

This is Italian cooking at its best. It's basically pasta with cheese (ideally made from sheep's milk) and black pepper. It's a deceptively simple-sounding Roman dish, but the secret is all in the technique; you can search Youtube to see an expert doing it.

Add the spaghetti to a large pot of salted boiling water and cook until *al dente*. Drain the pasta over a bowl so you keep the cooking water.

Return the spaghetti to the pan and mix in the olive oil and some black pepper. Add two ladlefuls of cooking water and sprinkle on the Pecorino. Toss it into the spaghetti using two forks; if it's too dry, add a bit more pasta water, and if there is too much water, add more Pecorino. Give it a really good grind of pepper, and keep tossing. What you are trying to achieve is a creamy soft sauce: to start with there will be lumps of melted cheese and the water will separate out, but if you keep on tossing it will come together. Give it yet more black pepper, toss again, and serve immediately.

400g spaghetti

1 tbsp olive oil

160g Pecorino Romano, grated

freshly ground black pepper

Pasta Frittata

Serves 4-6

600g spaghetti

3 tbsp olive oil

6 free range eggs

150g Parmesan,
finely grated

sea salt

freshly ground black pepper

This is a cheap, easy dinner, and it's great for using left-overs. The recipe below is for a frittata using freshly cooked pasta, as is popular in Cookie for lunch. At home we use any left-over spaghetti, sauce and all, to make it – just weigh what you have left over and use an egg per 100g. The end result will vary depending on the pasta sauce, but tomato-based dishes work particularly well with egg.

First, cook your pasta in plenty of salted water until *al dente*. Drain the pasta and put it back in the pan with a tablespoon of the olive oil, some salt, and a good grind of black pepper. Leave it to cool right down.

Break the eggs into a bowl big enough to hold the pasta, and mix in the Parmesan and some salt and pepper. When the pasta is cool, add it to the eggs and mix thoroughly, making sure all the pieces are well coated with egg. Heat the remaining oil in a cast iron or non-stick frying pan over a high flame. When the oil is good and hot, pour in the frittata mixture, give the pan a good shake to help it settle, and turn the heat down to medium. Cover the pan with a lid or a large plate. Cook it for 2-3 minutes, and then run a knife or spatula around the edge of the pan to loosen the frittata. Invert in onto the plate, and slide the frittata back into the frying pan, runny side down. Scrape in any uncooked remnants left on the plate. Cook it for a further 1-2 minutes, pressing down with a spatula, until it's firm and golden brown.

Serve it immediately.

Fishcakes

Serves 4

You find regional variations of fishcakes all over the world, as they're an economical way of stretching fish a bit further. These are our Italian-style ones.

*A word on capers: capers are a natural partner for fishcakes. They are the buds of the perennial deciduous **Capparis Spinosa** plant, which are picked just before they flower. The buds are categorized by their size and can be pickled or stored in salt – we tend to use salted ones as the flavour is preserved better. The best capers in the world, in our opinion, come from Panetella in Sicily, which is where Cookie imports from.*

Preheat the oven to 180°C.

Wash and dry the fish, and then rub it with olive oil. Place it in a steamer, if you have one, or in a colander covered with foil. Fill two pans, one large and one small, with plenty of water, add a teaspoon of salt to each and bring them up to the boil. Hardboil one of the eggs in the small pan for 10 minutes. Add the potatoes to the large pan and, when it comes to the boil again, turn the heat down to a gentle simmer. After 4 minutes, put the fish in its steamer or colander over the potato pan and cook for a further 8 minutes. The potatoes should be soft by then; if they're not, remove the fish and finish the potatoes. Drain the potatoes and mash them in the pan with a pinch of salt and the olive oil.

Remove any skin and bones from the fish, and flake the flesh into the potatoes. Add the lemon zest, the parsley, and the capers and mix well. Finely chop the hard-boiled egg and stir that in, too. Season the mixture (but bear in mind that smoked fish will be salty, so if that's what you're using you might want to omit the salt altogether).

Shape the mixture into 8 rounds. (They can be frozen at this point). Put the flour in one bowl, a lightly beaten egg in a second bowl, and the breadcrumbs in a third. Dip each fishcake into the flour, into the egg, and finally into the breadcrumbs, making sure they're fully covered. Then put them on a greased baking tray and bake for 20 minutes.

100g fish (any kind you like)

1 tbsp olive oil, plus more for rubbing

300g potatoes, peeled and quartered

2 free range eggs

zest of 1 unwaxed lemon

a handful of flat-leaf parsley, finely chopped

1 tbsp capers, rinsed

1 tbsp plain flour

100g breadcrumbs

sea salt

freshly ground black pepper

Zarzuela de Mariscos

Serves 4-6

1kg white fish and shellfish

4 tbsp olive oil

1 large onion,
finely chopped

a piece of chorizo or cured
ham, diced (optional)

2 garlic cloves,
finely chopped

400g plum tomatoes

2 bay leaves

2 strands saffron

50g almonds or hazelnuts,
ground

1 tbsp fennel seeds

200ml white wine

1l fish stock
(or you can use water)

a dash of Pernod or Ricard

1 sprig of thyme, leaves only

A small handful of flat-leaf
parsley, roughly chopped

sea salt

freshly ground black pepper

Fish stew is another use-up dish – you can use whatever fish you find, with the exception of oily fish like mackerel, which are much better grilled or baked.

Clean and prepare your fish and shellfish, and cut the white fish into bite-size pieces.

In a heavy pan large enough to take all of the fish, heat the olive oil and sauté the onions until they're soft and transparent. Add the chorizo or ham, if you are using them, and brown it all a bit. Then stir in the garlic, tomatoes, bay leaves, saffron, ground nuts and fennel seeds, and bring the mixture to a boil.

Turn down the heat and leave it to simmer ever so gently for 10 minutes. Pour in the white wine, followed by the fish stock and a slug of Pernod. Season it and simmer for another 10 minutes. (If you want, you can freeze it at this point).

Lastly, add the fish, the thyme and the parsley. Cover the pan and let the stew simmer for 10 minutes, and then turn off the heat and leave it to sit for another 5, allowing all the flavours to meld. Serve with some crusty bread to dip in the sauce.

The Stornoway Tower

Serves 1

Going out for breakfast in Italy means great coffee, and possibly a freshly squeezed orange juice, but the food is, at best, a dry cornetto (think of a croissant, only not quite as good). So, brunch seems to us to be a meal that Scotland does well. Our black pudding comes from Stornoway and was the inspiration behind The Tower. Our bacon is home cured by our local friend, the owner of Gusto and Relish.

The trick to poaching the perfect egg is to use a large volume of water and vinegar, relative to the egg – the proportions should be 70% water to 30% vinegar. So, get a deep saucepan, put in, say, 350ml of water and 150ml of vinegar, and it bring up to the boil.

Crack one of the eggs into a bowl which is shallow enough for dipping in your slice of bread. Lightly mix the egg with a fork and season it well. Start grilling the bacon and black pudding.

Heat the oil and butter gently in a pan, taking care not to burn the butter. Dip the bread in the beaten egg and fry it on both sides. Then drain it on kitchen paper and keep it warm on a plate. Your water and vinegar should be boiling by now, so turn it down to a simmer, and carefully crack in the remaining egg. Cook it for 2 minutes and remove with a slotted spoon.

Now make your tower: use the French toast as the base, and then build up your tower using the black pudding, then the bacon and, finally, your perfectly poached egg. This is a good time to get out the Drumnadrochit Tomato Ketchup (page 63).

2 free range eggs

2 rashers of unsmoked bacon

1 thick slice of Stornoway black pudding

1 tbsp olive oil

1 tbsp butter

1 slice of good quality bread

red wine vinegar for poaching

sea salt

freshly ground black pepper

The Veggie Volcano

Serves 1

3 tbsp olive oil

400g tinned plum tomatoes

¼ tsp dried chilli flakes

¼ tsp salt

1 beef tomato

1 large portobello
mushroom

1 slice of vegetarian haggis

2 free range eggs

1 slice of good quality bread

1 tbsp butter

red wine vinegar
for poaching

sea salt

freshly ground black pepper

This is the vegetarian version of The Stornoway Tower.

Start off with the sauce. Put 2 tablespoons of the oil into a small pan over a medium heat. Add the plum tomatoes, chilli flakes and salt and simmer it all, smashing the tomatoes with a wooden spoon. Cook for 10 minutes or so, until the sauce has a jammy consistency, and then blitz it with a hand-blender.

Cut a thick slice from the beef tomato, and it season lightly. Put the tomato slice and the mushroom on a grill pan, drizzle them with oil and put them under a hot grill for 5 minutes, until both are lightly cooked. Keep them warm on a plate.

The haggis should be cooked whole, and then sliced. We boil them, which is the traditional method, but most are also easy to cook in the microwave.

Break one of the eggs into a bowl which is shallow enough for dipping in your bread. Lightly beat the egg with a fork and season it well. Melt the butter and the remaining tablespoon of oil in a frying pan, and then dip the bread in the egg and fry until it's golden brown on both sides. Drain the bread on kitchen paper, and then keep it warm with the tomato and mushroom.

Poach the remaining egg in a pan of boiling water and vinegar (70% water to 30% vinegar) for 2 minutes, and then remove it with a slotted spoon.

Now make your veggie volcano: use your French toast as a base, then add the grilled tomato, then the mushroom, then the haggis and, finally, the poached egg. Cover the volcano with a good helping of the hot tomato sauce and serve immediately.

Gingerbread

Serves 12-15

Reality says our student son is unlikely to bake much, but in case he does, we picked a cake that improves with time rather than needing to be eaten right away. This is good for quite a few people, and it lasts for at least the rest of the week.

The recipe came from a Women's Institute book of wartime cakes and is pretty economical. I've added the stem ginger, but it's cheaper (and fine) without.

Preheat the oven to 170°C. Grease and line your tin.

Put the treacle, syrup, sugar and butter into a large pan and heat it really gently, stirring regularly, until the sugar has dissolved. Take the pan off the heat and stir in the grated ginger and stem ginger.

Sift the flour into a large bowl and add the bicarbonate of soda and the dry spices. Make a well in the middle. Put the milk in a jug, stir in the egg, and then pour it all into the warm syrupy butter mixture in the pan, stirring with a wooden spoon. Finally, pour the contents of the pan into the well in the flour, and mix everything thoroughly – it will be a rather runny, deep brown batter.

Pour the batter into the prepared tin and bake for 1-1 $\frac{1}{4}$ hours. It's ready when a skewer comes out clean.

Leave the gingerbread to cool in the tin on a wire rack, then remove it from the tin and wrap it in greaseproof paper and foil. Store it in an airtight container for two days before eating.

175g treacle

175g golden syrup

175g dark brown muscovado sugar

175g butter

1cm fresh ginger, grated

5 pieces of stem ginger, chopped

350g plain flour ('00' if possible)

$\frac{3}{4}$ tsp bicarbonate of soda

1 tbsp ground ginger

1 tsp mixed spice

150ml whole milk

1 free range egg, beaten

20cm square, 8cm deep cake tin

Limoncello Cake

Serves 8-10

Cake

125g butter, softened

175g caster sugar

2 free range eggs

zest of 2 unwaxed lemons

175g self-raising flour

4 tbsp milk

Topping

5 tbsp limoncello

or

100g icing sugar

3tbsp lemon juice

23 x 13 x 7cm loaf tin

This is a cake for winter, when lemons are in season. Nature made them ripen then to keep up our vitamin C and prevent colds, and limoncello must have some sort of medicinal quality as well.

First, make your limoncello (see page 29), or buy some from Cookie. Then, start baking. This cake can be (and has been) made by 2 year olds. It's a one bowl, mixer on, into the tin job. It's less mess than any ready-made mixes, and there are no packets to throw in the landfill.

Preheat oven to 180°C. Grease and line a loaf tin.

With an electric whisk, cream the butter and sugar until fluffy. Keep whisking as you add in the eggs, one by one, and then the lemon zest, the flour and, lastly, the milk to get a nice dropping consistency. Pour the batter into the tin and bake it for 40 minutes, or until a skewer comes out clean. Cool the cake in the tin on a wire rack.

When it's cold, you can give it whatever treatment the occasion deserves. While the cake is still in the tin, stick lots of holes in it with a skewer. Then, either pour over the limoncello, or heat icing sugar and lemon juice together to make a smooth syrup and pour that over. Take the cake out of the tin when all the limoncello (or syrup) has soaked in.

Granola

This is a Cookie favourite. It keeps for 4 weeks if kept in an airtight box, and it is great as a breakfast cereal, on yoghurt or even just as a snack on its own. We think it ticks a lot of boxes on the healthy eating front, as it's got nuts, seeds and all those essential oils and vitamins. Apart from its tastiness, the main attraction for someone cooking for themselves is its longevity. Make it once and you have a supply for weeks ahead and can avoid those all too quickly finished, full of sugar breakfast cereals. And price-wise, it's so much cheaper to make your own – do the maths.

This granola is also really flexible. The nuts are interchangeable: peanuts are the cheapest option, and you just use the same quantity. Chocolate works well: just add 30g of good quality cocoa. I also like an all fruit version, using 250g of various dried fruit instead of the almonds, and adding it at the end with the raisins.

This recipe is the basic one, and it makes the perfect amount to fit in a 3.9l tupperware cereal dispenser boxes.

Preheat the oven to 160°C and lightly grease 2 big baking trays.

Put the apple into a small pan with enough water to come about a quarter of the way up the fruit. Cook the apple gently until it's soft, and then stir it with a wooden spoon to make a rough puree. Leave it to cool.

Get out the biggest bowl you have, and put in the apple puree and all of the other ingredients apart from the raisins. Mix it all up thoroughly, and then spread it evenly onto your baking trays in a layer about 2cm thick. Bake the granola for 40 minutes, carefully stirring it half way through to stop anything burning.

Leave it to cool – if you can, leave it overnight in the turned-off oven. Add the raisins (and any other fruit) and store the granola in your airtight container. Enjoy.

1 large cooking apple (weighing about 200g), peeled, cored and chopped

450g porridge oats (the large oat type if possible)

120g sunflower seeds

130g sesame seeds

5 tbsp runny honey

1 tbsp sea salt

2 tbsp good quality olive oil

100g soft brown sugar

2 tsp cinnamon

½ tsp nutmeg, grated

1 tsp ginger

¼ tsp allspice

5 tbsp syrup (a great quality one such as cranberry syrup, or the cheaper golden syrup)

250g whole almonds

300g raisins

Elliott's Bread Rolls

Makes about 20

150ml tepid water

*1 tbsp dried yeast
(or 30g of fresh)*

1 tsp sugar

1 tbsp butter, softened

500g strong white flour

*1 tsp cooking salt
(not sea salt)*

200ml tepid milk

extra flour for kneading

1 free range egg, beaten

50g poppy or sesame seeds

Rolls are a good way of having freshly baked bread, and they are a little more economical for one. They also need less time in the oven, and they are easy to freeze in small quantities – just wrap them individually once they're cooked and cooled.

Activate your yeast as normal: put 100ml of the tepid water into a jug and stir in the yeast and the sugar. Leave it for 15 minutes or so, until a frothy head has developed.

In a large bowl, rub the butter into the flour, add the salt, and stir in the milk and the remaining 50ml of water. Mix it with your hands to bring the dough together, then turn it out onto a floured surface and knead it for 10 minutes or so, until it's smooth and elastic. Put the dough back into a floured bowl, cover it with a dish cloth and leave it to prove somewhere warm (about an hour), until it has doubled in size.

Punch the dough down, and knead it for another 5 minutes. Then divide the dough into small, clementine-sized balls, and roll each one in your hands to get a nice, smooth finish. Place the balls, spaced out well, on a greased baking tray. Cover them with a cloth and leave them to prove for another 30 minutes or so. Turn your oven to 190°C in the meantime.

When the oven's hot and the rolls have doubled in size, brush them gently with the beaten egg and scatter over some seeds. Bake them at 190°C for 12 minutes, or until golden and hollow-sounding when you tap one on the bottom. Leave them to cool on a wire rack.

Domenico

Domenico is a purist. If we go out for dinner, our children truly expect that we will have to look at 5 different restaurants before he deems one acceptable, even if we are all starving. The end result is always quality – he never compromises.

This part of the book is all about recipes that are meant to impress. This is the section to come to when you want to put together those special menus and experiment a little with top quality ingredients. None of these recipes are at all complicated, but there is a focus on luxury and things you might want to cook for important occasions or celebrations.

Finding specialist ingredients, or working out which wines are best suited to a particular meal, requires focus, like finding the right restaurant. Whatever he is doing, Domenico is focused. He is the creative force behind Cookie and all that it does. Passionate, single-minded and capable, Domenico always comes up with an excellent end result. These recipes reflect his approach to quality.

Big Fish (Atlantic Halibut with Roast Potatoes)

1 whole halibut, size depending

potatoes (choose a waxy one like Charlotte, and you need enough to cover the fish completely when sliced)

olive oil

1-2 sprigs of rosemary, finely chopped

sea salt

freshly ground black pepper

One of the great fish from Scottish waters is the Atlantic Halibut. These are flat fish which can grow to considerable sizes and are now being sustainably farmed on the Isle of Gigha, where Cookie gets its halibut from. It's an amazing success story of the Scottish fishery industry, which we visited on a family holiday.

We think this wonderful fish is best cooked simply to let the flavour and texture come through: pan-cook it or bake it but, most importantly, don't overcook it.

There are various ways to lock in flavour: it can be baked in salt, in foil or, in this case, sealed in by potatoes which makes it difficult to overcook. In Europe, pre-filleting is uncommon, and a fish like this would be presented to guests for their approval before it is cooked.

When choosing your fish, look for it to be firm and resilient to the touch, with bright eyes and shiny skin. It should not smell too fishy. Halibut are big-boned fish, so removing the bones is simple. Ask the fishmonger to gut it only. The size depends on how many people are eating it, and what's available, so ask your fishmonger for advice, and reckon on giving people about 225g per person. In this recipe we cook this fish whole, so remember the size of your oven or bring the baking tray you'll use with you, just in case.

If you can't find a whole halibut, you can make this with turbot or plaice.

Preheat the oven to 190°C. First, slice your potatoes: if you have a slicer, great – your life will be easy! If you don't, take your time: we are looking for the potatoes to be sliced into rounds about 3-4mm thick, and the more consistent the thickness, the more even the cooking. If you are using a small fish such as plaice, parboil the potatoes whole for 7 minutes, and then leave them to cool a moment before slicing them.

Line your baking tray with silver foil. Spread a layer of potato slices across this, and then give them a quick drizzle of olive oil and sprinkle over some rosemary. Place the fish on top and, working up from the tail, cover the fish entirely in overlapping potato slices. You can spend your time working out the best design, but make sure you have covered the entire fish, including the sides. Drizzle it with olive oil, sprinkle it with more rosemary and give it a good dusting with sea salt. Cook it in the oven until the potatoes are golden brown .

Lobsters at a Wedding (Lobster in Tomato Sauce)

Serves 4

2 lobsters

4 tbsp olive oil

2 garlic cloves, crushed on the back of your knife

1 onion, finely chopped

2 dried red chilli peppers

2 x 400g tins of quality tomatoes

½ a glass of Cognac

500g spaghetti (dried, not fresh)

a few leaves of basil

This is the recipe we used for our wedding. We hired a big marquee, put an industrial kitchen out back and cooked for our pals. We bought two crates of oysters to start and then made this lip-smacking, finger-licking recipe of Scottish lobsters, **Homarus gammarus**. Smaller, firmer and tastier than their North American counterparts, they always make me think of the Scottish national flag because of their blue colour. Scottish lobsters are not as expensive as you think they would be, although I'd avoid buying them during the Christmas season as the prices are inflated. One of the reasons I think people avoid them is the perceived difficulty in cooking fresh lobsters. Don't worry – it is easy. Choose a lobster which feels heavy for its size, is lively and has a straight tail.

Regarding the tomato sauce, I'll say it again: there is no shame in using good quality tinned tomatoes. I always look on the back of the tin to find out where they are from. The letters 'SA' or 'NO' (Salerno and Nocera Inferiore-Gragnano) bring a definite purchase, as this is the area Bruno comes from, which is famous for plum tomatoes. You will never get the same flavour out of a hot house tomato from Holland, fresh or otherwise.

Fill a wide, deep pan half way with water and bring it to the boil. Pop your lobsters in. The cooking time depends on their size, and I always undercook them a bit as we will be finishing this off in a sauce – 8 minutes should be plenty. Take them out but don't throw away the water! That is your stock, which you'll use in the sauce and to cook the pasta.

To prepare the lobster meat, break off the claws and the legs. Find the cross on the back of the shell body, insert your fantastically sharp kitchen knife at this point, and firmly cut down to the end of the tail. Then turn the lobster around and cut up through the head: you'll have two halves of lobster with all the meat accessible.

Heat the olive oil in a large, shallow pan. Cook the garlic and onion over a medium-low heat until the onions are soft and transparent. Discard the garlic and put in the chilli peppers, the tomatoes and a ladleful of the stock. Bring the mixture to the boil and simmer it for 15 minutes, or until the sauce starts to thicken and change consistency. Add your lobster halves, shells and all, and pour in the Cognac. Cook it all gently for another 5 minutes. Meanwhile, bring the pan of lobster stock to the boil and use it to cook the spaghetti, draining the pasta a couple of minutes before it is done. Turn the heat down under the sauce, add the drained, not quite cooked spaghetti, and leave to cook for another couple of minutes, until the pasta is *al dente* and has absorbed some of the sauce.

Decorate with fresh basil, put on a bib, and eat – licking your fingers as you go.

Acqua Pazza Crazy Water Fish

Serves 2

1 whole bream or bass

a small bunch of flat-leaf parsley

2 ½ garlic cloves, crushed on the back of your knife

olive oil

2 tomatoes, roughly chopped

½ dried red chilli (optional)

150ml white wine

sea salt

freshly ground black pepper

Crazy water, or 'acqua pazza', is a way of poaching fish. It has its origins on the west coast of Italy and has become well-known in holiday destinations such as Capri and Ponza.

This is poached fish with flavour. It is an incredibly easy and healthy way to cook, and perfect for people on diets.

You can use most white fish for this – we like to use black bream. We cook the fish whole as it adds to the flavour; you can ask your fishmonger to clean, gut and descale it. We have never understood the obsession with fillets in the UK. Learning to eat whole fish is a skill for life.

Preheat your oven to 200°C.

Clean, gut and descale the fish (or get your fishmonger to do it for you). Put a little salt, a parsley stalk and half of a crushed garlic clove in the cavity.

Pour a little olive oil in the bottom of an ovenproof dish. Put the fish in, and scatter around the chopped tomatoes, the crushed garlic cloves (broken up into pieces), and some chopped parsley. Season it and crumble in a little chilli pepper if you like.

Now pour in the white wine, and add enough water to come up just below the middle line of the fish. Bake it for around 20 to 25 minutes. To check it is cooked, pull on a fin – if it comes away easily, it is ready.

Use a slotted spoon to move the fish on to a plate, and then peel off the skin and take the flesh from the bones. Put the flesh back into the sauce in the oven dish and serve it hot or cold.

Linguine Vongole

Serves 4

This is a classic of southern Italian cuisine. Its greatness lies in its simplicity – it is one of those dishes (like an omelette) which, if done right, can be heaven, and, if not, can be a disaster. The key things are top quality ingredients and timing: it needs to be cooked and served immediately. The secret to achieving an almost buttery consistency is in finishing the pasta in the clam sauce.

Rinse and clean the clams under running water and put them in a pan. Cover them with water, add a couple of handfuls of salt, then put the lid on and leave them to purge. After a couple of hours, drain then clams and give them a good rinse to get rid of any of the grit.

Heat the olive oil in a large, heavy saucepan over a medium heat, and then throw in the clams and the wine. Cover and cook them until all the shells are all open. Discard any that stubbornly stay closed, and add the garlic, chilli and lemon zest. You can take the pan off the heat at this point and remove any shells that the clams have dropped out of.

Meanwhile, bring a large pan of water to the boil with plenty of salt. Cook the pasta, but drain it a couple of minutes before it's done. Turn on the heat under the clams again and stir in the pasta. Continue to cook it until *al dente* or slightly chewy. Then, toss through the roughly chopped parsley, drizzle it all with a little good olive oil and serve it quickly, while hot, with the basil to decorate.

750g surf clams

4 tbsp extra virgin olive oil

100ml dry white wine

3 garlic cloves, finely chopped

1 fresh medium-hot red chilli, finely chopped

zest of 1/2 an unwaxed lemon

500g linguine (dried, not fresh)

a small bunch of flat-leaf parsley, roughly chopped

a few leaves of basil

sea salt

Porchetta

Serves 8-10 (and leaves some for the week's sandwiches)

3 sprigs of rosemary, leaves finely chopped

a small bunch of flat-leaf parsley, finely chopped

a small bunch of sage, finely chopped

1 tbsp fennel seeds

4 garlic cloves, crushed on the back of your knife

4 or 5 chicken livers (optional), roughly chopped

zest of ½ an unwaxed lemon

3kg pork shoulder, butterfly cut with the skin left on

sea salt

freshly ground black pepper

kitchen twine

Porchetta is fast food in Rome, prefect for builders and hungry architects. A slice of bread from Genzano, porchetta with lots of stuffing please, a glass of white wine from the Castelli Romani... and you will be smiling. And all of these preferably from the little stand near San Giovanni, or Er Buchetto on Via del Viminale.

The whole pig versions of porchetta look like something from a medieval dinner table, but they are relatively easy to replicate at home using pork shoulder. Ask your butcher for a butterfly cut, leaving the skin on.

Preheat the oven to the hottest temperature it will go – 240°C is a good start.

Crush the herbs with the fennel seeds in a large pestle and mortar. Add in the garlic and chicken livers (if using them), and continue crushing so you get a good paste. Finally, stir in the lemon zest.

Lay the pork out on a board and rub salt and pepper into both sides. Turn it skin side down and spread the herby stuffing mixture evenly across the meat's surface. Roll the pork up tightly and tie it with some lengths of kitchen twine to hold it firmly in place.

Lightly grease a large roasting tray. If you have a rack to sit the pork on, so much the better, as you can then catch the fat and use it to baste the joint as it cooks. Otherwise, lay whole carrots across the middle of the roasting tray and put the pork on top, skin side up. Drizzle it with some olive oil to get the crackling going. Give it another liberal sprinkling of salt and pepper, and put it into the very hot oven. After 10 minutes, baste it and continue roasting for another 10 minutes; you should see the beginning of some crackling. Turn down the oven to 180°C and cook for 3 ½-4 hours, basting the joint occasionally. For extra moistness, I sometimes pour in a glass of rich red wine half way through the cooking time. Take the pork out of the oven when it's fully done and leave it to rest for 10 minutes while you boil up the roasting tray juices for gravy.

Serve it hot for Sunday lunch and use the left-overs cold for school sandwiches.

Rabbit with Juniper

Serves 4

Rabbit is one the healthiest and most forgotten lean meats of the United Kingdom. It is so much tastier than chicken, and it doesn't suffer from the same problems of large scale commercial production. We use wild rabbit which is much smaller that the commercially farmed varieties. They live in colonies on sandy soil and farmers are happy to cull them to avoid the damage they can cause to their crops. If you look into it, rabbit is one of the most ethically sourced meats around. Ask your butcher to joint the rabbit, or do it yourself – but take the time to do it carefully as the bones are very fragile and can shatter easily.

You can substitute chicken for rabbit in this recipe if you like.

a whole rabbit, jointed into 6 pieces

2 garlic cloves crushed

2 sprigs of rosemary

1 sprig of sage

1 bay leaf

8 juniper berries

125ml white wine vinegar

125ml Cookie white wine (or another dry white wine)

plain flour

4 tbsp olive oil

sea salt

freshly ground black pepper

Season the rabbit pieces with salt and pepper and put them in a bowl with the crushed garlic cloves, rosemary, sage, bay and juniper berries. Pour over the vinegar and wine, and leave it to marinate for at least 4 hours.

Preheat the oven to 180°C. Remove the rabbit from the marinade, pat it dry and dust it with flour. Heat the olive oil in a wide-bottomed, ovenproof casserole, and seal the meat, turning it so it browns on all sides. Add in the garlic and the herbs from the marinade, and continue cooking it all for another few minutes. Pour in the remaining marinade liquid and bring it to a gentle boil. Bake it, covered, for an hour.

Timballo

Serves 10

Pastry
300g '00' or plain flour
150g unsalted butter
5 tbsp of ice cold water (approximately)

Filling
olive oil
1 tbsp butter or lard
1 onion, finely chopped
1 carrot, finely chopped
1 stalk of celery, finely chopped
200g pork shoulder, cubed
200g stewing steak, cubed
50g mushrooms, roughly chopped
400g tin plum tomatoes
60ml Marsala
¼ tsp nutmeg, grated
400g macaroni or rigatoni
250ml good chicken stock
2 hardboiled free range eggs, sliced
100g prosciutto, torn into pieces
150g Pecorino, grated
sea salt
freshly ground black pepper

2l pudding basin (or pyrex bowl)

The timballo is a southern Italian dish which can be cooked in many different forms with varying ingredients, but it always uses pasta as a base. Originating from the courts of Sicily and Naples, timballi became particularly fashionable in Naples from the 18th century onwards. Timballi are baked in a mould in the oven so that when they're turned out they hold their shape. Some versions (like this one) have a pastry case and some simply bake the pasta filling. Rich in flavour and ingredients, they often appear on the Sunday dinner table, or make up part of a picnic as they hold their firm shape so well. This is the classic Neapolitan version. It's fine to use shop bought pastry; you need about 500g.

First, if you're not using shop-bought, make the pastry. Sift the flour into a large bowl and then rub in the butter with your fingertips until it resembles fine breadcrumbs. Add the water a tablespoon at a time, stirring it in with a table knife, until the pastry starts to come together. Knead it very lightly until it you have a smooth ball of dough, and then wrap it in cling film and put it in the fridge until you're ready to roll it out.

Now make the ragù, starting with a soffrito base. Put a large casserole over a medium-low heat, and pour in enough olive oil to line the pan. Add the butter or lard and melt it. Then stir in the onion, carrot and celery and cook until it's soft but not at all brown. Turn the heat up to medium and add the pork and beef. Give it a good stir and fry until the meat is sealed on all sides. Put in the mushrooms and tomatoes, and then the Marsala and nutmeg. Fill up your empty tomato tin with water and pour that in too, then it season well and bring it all to the boil. Cover and simmer it on a very low heat for a couple of hours.

When the ragù is cooked, turn your oven on to 200°C. Cook whatever pasta you're using in a large pan of boiling water, with the chicken stock added for flavour. Drain the pasta when *al dente*. In a very large bowl, mix everything together: the ragù, the pasta, the eggs, the prosciutto and the grated Pecorino. Taste for seasoning.

On a floured work surface, roll out two thirds of your pastry to about 5mm thick, and use it to line your greased pudding basin. Pour in the pasta filling, and then roll out the final third of pastry to make the lid. Put it on the top, crimp the edges together firmly, and then cut a small vent in the middle.

Bake the timballo for 35 minutes and then turn it out onto a large plate to serve. It will firm up on cooling.

Roast Fennel

Serves 4-6 as a side dish

4 large fennel bulbs

250ml milk

3 tbsp olive oil

2 tbsp breadcrumbs

3 tbsp Parmesan, grated

sea salt

freshly ground black pepper

We use fennel in many different ways. The seeds are good for making a relaxing tea and can be used in sauces and stuffing; they go particularly well with pork dishes. The fresh leaves are a good substitute for dill, and they are great as a flavour for bruschetta on sourdough bread. Cultivated fennel is an autumn vegetable with an anise flavour: it's delicious raw, thinly sliced with just a drizzle of olive oil and sprinkle of sea salt; and it's also delicious roasted, which changes the flavour so much it's almost another vegetable.

Preheat the oven to 180°C.

Trim the fennel, taking a slice off the base and cutting off the coarse green tops, and then cut it into quarters lengthwise. Put the fennel into a pan of boiling water and boil for 10 minutes, but don't overcook them – they should still be firm.

Drain the fennel quarters and lay them in a single layer in a casserole dish. Pour over the milk, drizzle them with oil, and then sprinkle them with the breadcrumbs and Parmesan. Season the fennel well and pop them in the oven for 30 minutes, or until they're crisp and golden brown on top.

Cavolo Nero and Winter Greens

Serves 4

Here is a method to sweat your winter greens in a pan rather than boiling them and losing some of the flavours.

Chop the greens, throwing away the base of the stems which can be too hard compared to the leaves. Set them aside.

In a large frying pan, preferably with a lid, put in 1-2 tablespoons of olive oil, the garlic and the chilli pepper. If you like, add some chopped pancetta and fry it all gently, until the garlic is transparent and the pancetta is starting to brown at the edges. Add the greens and a little water and cook, covered, on a moderate heat for 5-10 minutes according to the quantity and type of green you're using. If needed, add a little water to keep it moist. When the greens are tender, serve.

450g cavolo nero or winter greens

olive oil

1 garlic clove, finely chopped

1 dried chilli pepper

a piece of pancetta, chopped (optional)

Panzanella

Serves 4

*about 250g left-over
dry bread*

1 tsp red wine vinegar

½ red onion, finely chopped

*½ small cucumber, peeled
and roughly chopped*

4 very good tomatoes

good quality olive oil

sea salt

Dried bread is a fact of life, but it should never go to waste as it has many uses. From our dried left-overs of bread, we make breadcrumbs to use in stuffings, in gratin dishes, as a part of our mix for burgers – or we make this classic Tuscan salad. We are talking here about real bread, not the pan loaf variety that turns into aerated wafer crisps in the toaster. Our family cannot touch the stuff. After a life-time of eating homemade bread, the commercial stuff is impossible to eat.

Panzanella can be found in many varieties throughout Italy, each one using slightly varying ingredients. It is poor man's food – using up the scraps – so the quantities are deliberately vague. Here is the classic version with some suggestions for variations.

Soak the dry bread in 200ml of water with a little red wine vinegar added, and then leave it to drain well in a colander. You don't want any water to separate into the finished salad so leave it draining while you're chopping everything else for the salad.

Finely chop the red onion. The ones from Tropea in Calabria are the most famous Italian red onion variety: sweet, not too harsh, and perfect for eating raw. If you want to take the edge off less subtle onions, you can soak them in water and red wine vinegar for an hour before adding them to the salad.

Peel and roughly chop the cucumber. If possible, look for the small ones with rough skin (but take the skin off). This recipe is older than the New World, and cucumber was the star of the show before the tomato arrived on the scene.

You need the best tomatoes you can find for this, so look for ripe vine tomatoes. Dutch hot house tomatoes are useless and you will only be disappointed with the results. If you are stuck, buy cherry tomatoes and roast them for 20 minutes with some garlic and a little oregano to intensify their flavour. Whatever tomatoes you're using, chop them into big chunks.

Mix the bread, the onions, the cucumber and the tomatoes in your serving bowl, and dress with the best olive oil you can buy. Season the panzanella well with sea salt. Once all your ingredients are mixed, let it sit in the fridge for the flavours to infuse into the bread.

While that is the hard-core, classic Tuscan version, you can always branch out and experiment with other ones. Try adding some black olives, or some tuna and rinsed capers with a squeeze of lemon and a sprinkling of fresh oregano. Sometimes we add a chopped boiled egg.

Bunet

Serves 10

300g caster sugar

900ml milk

250g amaretti biscuits
(the hard type)

8 free range eggs

50g bitter cocoa powder

50g ground hazelnuts
(make sure they are really
fine – you can do this in a
coffee grinder)

100ml espresso coffee

50ml Fernet Branca
or Amaro

dark chocolate and fresh
mint to serve

a 2lb loaf or terrine tin
(about 30 x 15 x 8cm)

This is a chocolate pudding for adults.

The first time we ate this pudding was in Turin at a curious restaurant on the first floor of a suburban apartment building. From the darkness of the hallway, we were met by the patron – a large lady, fussily dressed, who opened the door into a bright restaurant with waiters dressed in white buzzing around. It was a dream-like experience. The pudding was Bunet, and it became an obsession.

Preheat the oven to 170°C.

First, make your caramel. The trick to making it is the right pan and patience. You need a heavy-based pan, preferably stainless steel or aluminium, so you can see what is going on.

Gently warm your pan (overheat things at your peril!). Add 100g of the sugar and leave it to turn to liquid slowly, starting at the edges. When this happens (and only when this happens), give it a good shake, and leave it again until a quarter of the sugar has melted. Then, keeping it all on a medium-low heat, you can start to stir it gently with a wooden spoon until all the grains of sugar have melted. Within 10 minutes or so, you will have a lovely caramel the colour of dark amber. Take the pan off the heat and stir in 2 tablespoons of hot water from the tap – the caramel will bubble up, so take care, and keep stirring to remove any lumps. Pour it into your tin, and then tilt and tip it gently so the caramel completely covers the bottom and goes up the sides a bit.

Pour the milk into a saucepan on a low heat, and add the amaretti biscuits. Break the eggs into a large bowl, and then whisk in the remaining 200g of sugar until the mixture is light and frothy. Whisk in the cocoa, then the ground hazelnuts, then the coffee and, finally, the Fernet Branca or Amaro. Keep whisking until you have a perfectly smooth, chocolate-coloured mix.

Take your pan of hot milk and amaretti (by now soft and breaking up) and slowly pour the contents into the bowl with other ingredients and whisk it all thoroughly. Pour this custard into your caramel-lined tin. Put the tin into a roasting dish, and then add enough hot water into the roasting dish to come half way up the outside of the loaf tin. Put the whole thing into the oven, and bake it for 45 minutes. The pudding will be set but still wobbly – it will firm up a bit as it cools. Leave it to cool completely, and then turn it out onto a plate. Serve it in thick slices, with a grating of dark chocolate and a sprig of mint.

Pears in Red Wine

Serves 4

750ml red wine

2 cinnamon sticks

zest of ½ an unwaxed lemon

a pinch of ground cloves

1 vanilla pod (or 1 tsp of vanilla extract)

2 star anise

8 small firm pears, peeled but with the stalks left attached and intact

300g caster sugar

Pears do well in Scotland. These poached pears were a winning pudding for one of our Chef Wars, and the recipe turned out to be very simple and delicious. The best pears to use are slightly less ripe ones, so it's a great way of using up ones that remain stubbornly too hard to eat. If you're using riper fruits, simply reduce the cooking time. It also doesn't matter at all if the red wine you use is less than perfect or has been lying open for a day or two.

Pour the red wine into a large saucepan and bring it up to a simmer. Add the cinnamon sticks, the lemon zest, the ground cloves, the scraped insides of the vanilla pod (or the vanilla extract) and the star anise, and simmer it all for 5 minutes. Gently slide in the pears and the sugar, and then simmer it, covered, over a very low heat for 30 minutes. Take off the lid and simmer it for a further 30 minutes (or less if using ripe fruit), until the pears are absolutely tender.

Use a slotted spoon to carefully take the pears from the poaching liquor, and arrange them in a serving dish. They will be a beautiful deep purple. Strain the remaining red wine mixture and return it to the pan. Bring it to the boil and reduce it by half to a thick-ish syrup. Pour the red wine syrup over the pears and serve them warm or cold. They're delicious with crème fraîche.

Strawberries and Nasturtiums

Strawberries are well-known to taste great with pepper so, working on that principle, I figured peppery nasturtiums would be a perfect and beautiful compliment to them.

Nasturtiums are incredibly easy to grow: they don't worry about neglect and they give you back joy. They are good companion plants for cabbages, cauliflowers and zucchini in the allotment, as they attract aphids away from your veg. And they are perfect for all types of salads, adding colour and a peppery contrast.

strawberries

sugar

lemon juice

nasturtium flowers

Sprinkle the strawberries with sugar according to how sweet they are/your tooth is, and then squeeze on some lemon juice. This is all to taste, so do it bit by bit, and add a bit more sugar and lemon juice as you think it needs it. Toss the strawberries around to coat them well and then put them in the fridge. At the last minute before serving, decorate the strawberries with the flowers – and don't forget to tell people they can eat them!

Panpepato

Makes 4

100g sultanas

200g runny honey

150g dark chocolate (at least 70% cocoa solids)

100g almonds, roughly chopped

100g hazelnuts, roughly chopped

100g walnuts, roughly chopped

100g candied fruit (use cedro if you can find it)

2 tsp cinnamon

2 tsp nutmeg

2-3 tsp freshly ground black pepper, according to taste

200g plain flour

This is a traditional Umbrian recipe dating back as far as the Etruscans. It translates as 'peppered bread' and is a slightly spicier version of the better known panforte. Traditionally served at Christmas, it uses honey, dried fruit and nuts and is simplicity itself to make. Any candied fruit will work here: we always use cedro, which is a large lemon with no pulp. It's not easily available in the UK, but it is worth hunting out in specialist stores or online. If we don't have it, I use mixed peel or glace cherries. You can also vary the amount of pepper and spices to your own taste.

At Cookie we like a thin slice with coffee.

Preheat your oven to 180°C and lightly grease a baking tray.

Put the sultanas into a small bowl and cover them with hot water from a kettle so they plump up and soften.

In a bain marie, heat the honey until it boils. Break in the chocolate and stir it gently until it melts. Then add the nuts, the drained sultanas and the candied fruit and stir, keeping the mixture on a low heat. Sprinkle in the spices and black pepper, and mix it well.

Take the mixture off the heat and add 2 tablespoons of flour at a time, beating well after each addition. Continue to add flour until the mixture holds its shape (it's hard work!) and you can pick it up. You might not need the full 200g.

When it's stiff enough to hold, shape the panpepato into four little cakes (about 10cm in diameter) on your baking tray, and then bake them for 10 minutes. Leave them to cool on a wire rack.

This makes a beautiful and unusual Christmas present as it keeps for several weeks.

Amaretti Biscuits

Makes about 18

These were made for a Chef Wars event at Cookie. They make a very Italian finish to a meal, simple and perfect with a small glass of Vin Santo.

Preheat oven to 160°C and line a baking sheet with greaseproof paper.

In a large bowl, mix together the sugar, ground almonds, almond extract and lemon zest. Heat the honey in a bain marie until it is runny, and leave it to cool slightly. Whisk the egg whites in a metal bowl until they form soft peaks, and then whisk in the honey. With a metal spoon, gently fold the eggs into the almond mixture until everything is evenly mixed. You may need to add more ground almonds if it's too runny – the aim is for a dough you can shape.

Roll the dough into small walnut-sized balls between your palms (use about half a tablespoon of dough for each one). Roll each ball in the flaked almonds and put them on your baking sheet. Bake them for about 14 minutes, until they turn a light gold but have not browned.

Cool on a wire rack and dust them with icing sugar through a sieve before serving.

100g caster sugar

250g ground almonds

1 tsp almond extract

zest of 1 unwaxed lemon (preferably Amalfi)

2 tbsp honey (any type, but we use Ed's Honey)

2 free range egg whites

50g flaked almonds

icing sugar to dust

Index

VANGUARD SERIES

EDITOR: MARTIN WINDROW

THE M113 SERIES

Text by
SIMON DUNSTAN

Colour plates by
TERRY HADLER and DAVID E. SMITH

OSPREY PUBLISHING LONDON

Dedication
To Frederica

Published in 1983 by
Osprey Publishing Ltd
Member company of the George Philip Group
12–14 Long Acre, London WC2E 9LP
© Copyright 1983 Osprey Publishing Ltd
Reprinted 1983

British Library Cataloguing in Publication Data

Dunstan, Simon
  M113 series. — (Vanguard series; 34)
  1. United States. *Army*   2. Armored personnel
  carriers
  I. Title   II. Series
  623.74′75   UG4465

  ISBN 0-85045-495-6

Filmset in Great Britain
Printed in Hong Kong

Acknowledgements
The author's thanks are due to several individuals
and organisations for their help in the compilation of
this monograph. In particular, my thanks to George
J. Balin for the generous loan of reference material
and many photographs; to FMC Corporation for
providing a wealth of data; and to Steven J. Zaloga
for his unstinting assistance and the excellent scale
plan. I also wish to acknowledge the following:
Armor Magazine; Associations of Former ARVN
Personnel; Col. Raymond R. Battreall, US Army
(Retd); British Aerospace; Geoff Cornish; DMS;
Emerson Electric Company; Lt.Col. George Forty,
RTR (Retd); Christopher F. Foss; Maj. John P.
Graber, US Army; Paul Handel; Col. Stanley E.
Holtom, US Army (Retd); WO1 Doug Lennox,
RAAC; WO1 'Bluey' Lowe, RAAC; Richard
Ogorkiewicz; Tim Page; Lt. Gabriel Steinhardt,
IDF; Pierre Touzin; Soldier of Fortune Magazine;
11th Armored Cavalry Regiment; Tank-Automotive
Command (TACOM); Chief of Military History,
and Center of Military History, Washington DC;
US Army Exchange Officer, Bovington.

Introduction

Following the carnage of the Great War, innovatory military thinkers such as Col. J. F. C. Fuller and Capt. Basil Liddell Hart laid the intellectual foundations for the blitzkrieg tactics used so devastatingly by the Germans against Poland, France and the Soviet Union in the opening years of the Second World War. The essence of blitzkrieg lay in combining the shock action and mobile firepower of the tank with enhanced battlefield mobility for the infantryman, but early in the war no vehicle existed which integrated these functions to their full potentiality. The principal vehicle employed to bring troops on to the battlefield remained the vulnerable soft-skinned truck, while the armoured half-tracks used by the Germans (and later the Americans) were found to lack the cross-country mobility of tanks. This defect was mainly owing to their front wheels, which either followed the contours of the ground, slowing the vehicle down and giving the occupants a decidedly rough ride, or else bogged down in soft going and defiles. Worse, the open top of the troop compartment left its human cargo vulnerable to air-burst

The introduction of the M113 APC into the Mekong Delta in mid-1962, together with greater numbers of helicopters, greatly enhanced the mobility of ARVN forces in the swamps and rice paddies of the region. The inherent amphibious capability of the M113 proved invaluable among the many canals and watercourses of the waterlogged terrain. (Stanley Holtom)

artillery, strafing and grenade attack — the latter a particularly dangerous threat in the street-fighting of North-West Europe during 1944-5, when the interior of the vehicle was so often exposed to attack from the upper storeys of buildings. The solution was to enable the infantry to ride into battle in a completely enclosed, armoured, fully-tracked carrier.

M75 APC

Among the first such carriers developed in the post-war years was the M75. It was of welded steel construction, powered by an air-cooled six cylinder, horizontally opposed AO-895-4 Continental gasoline engine with CD-500-4 cross-drive transmission. The M75 was capable of lifting ten infantrymen plus commander and driver with their equipment at a combat loading of 41,500lbs. The carrier was originally developed and manufactured by the International Harvester Corporation, utilising automotive and

Deployed in its primary role of air defence, an M163A1 Vulcan named HOT CHOCOLATE protects a mechanised unit during manoeuvres in Germany, September 1978. Note the yellow 'bubble gum light' at hull rear, a mandatory warning device carried by all AFVs in Germany. (Pierre Touzin)

suspension components of the M41 Walker Bulldog light tank. The Food Machinery and Chemical Corporation (now FMC Corporation) was subsequently brought into the programme, and 1,729 vehicles were completed before production ceased in February 1954. The staggeringly high unit cost of over $100,000, however, was instrumental in bringing the assembly lines to a halt. In 1953 a few M75 APCs were used by the US Army in the Korean War (cf. Vanguard 27, *Armour of the Korean War*). Most M75s were subsequently transferred to the Belgian Army.

M59 APC

Even while production of the M75 was in progress, FMC had promoted a smaller, lighter vehicle costing half as much as the M75, and which also met the US Army requirement for amphibious operation. Design and development began in 1951 and the vehicle was standardised in December 1953 as the M59 Armored Personnel Carrier.

The M59 was powered by two liquid-cooled commercial truck engines coupled to a hydramatic transmission mounted directly to each engine. The use of commercially available engines and transmissions considerably reduced the cost of the vehicle, but the dual engine arrangement proved problematical, with insufficient power to enable the M59 to keep up with M48 tanks across country. Production of the M59 lasted from February 1954 until 1960. Just over 4,000 were built, including a 4.2-inch mortar version, the M84.

M113 APC

A new and challenging APC project, destined to become the longest running combat vehicle programme in the world, was initiated by the Army Ordnance Tank-Automotive Command (ATAC) (now the Tank-Automotive Command TACOM) in January 1956. The requirement was 'to provide a lightweight, armored personnel carrier for armor and infantry units capable of amphibious and air-drop operation, superior cross-country mobility and adaptation to multiple functions through applications of kits and/or modifications of its superstructure', under the designation Airborne, Armored, Multi-Purpose Vehicle Family.

The preliminary concept drawings were rapidly completed and a test bed (initially called the 'universal chassis') was built at ATAC within ninety days. It was powered by an Ordnance air-cooled engine, and featured rolled aluminium plate for the hull and as ballistic protection.

The use of aluminium for an armoured vehicle was an innovation. Facilities for producing aluminium had been underutilised since the Korean War and the manufacturers, seeking other uses for their product, had submitted samples of aluminium armour to the Army for test purposes. Trials revealed that in order to have comparable ballistic protection, aluminium armour weighed as much as conventional steel armour and had to be some three times as thick. However, since aluminium is considerably more rigid than steel for the same weight of metal, many structural braces can be eliminated, which reduces the overall weight of the vehicle and the number of man-hours involved in fabrication and welding, as well as increasing internal volume because of the absence of cross-members.

The test bed gave the ATAC engineers the opportunity to resolve numerous design problems such as the welding of aluminium plates, power plant design and performance, interior arrangements and weight limitations. The favourable outcome of these experiments led to the project being put out to tender in June 1956; during September the successful contender, the Ordnance Division of FMC Corporation, was contracted to develop and fabricate pilot models of the Airborne Multi-Purpose Vehicle Family.

Under this programme two distinct vehicle configurations were pursued. Five prototypes (T113) were constructed of aluminium armour and powered by air-cooled engines, and five of steel armour (T117) and powered by liquid-cooled engines. One each of the T113 and T117 ballistic hulls were manufactured and delivered to ATAC in 1957.

During this period many design alternatives were tried and tested using steel armour, aluminium armour, air-cooled engines, water-cooled engines, commercial transmissions and Ordnance

transmissions—when problems were encountered, other solutions were immediately sought, and the most promising designs and components were developed and evaluated through intensive hardware testing by FMC and ATAC.

Working in collaboration with Kaiser Aluminium and Chemical Corporation and using advanced welding techniques, FMC constructed the T113 with a combination of an aluminium hull and a Continental air-cooled engine providing the lightest weight configuration with superior ballistic protection. The more conventional steel hull design and Packard water-cooled engine was also built, since this evolved from the M59 APC and presented a low-risk option. The steering transmission used for both types was the Allison XTG-90 unit.

During testing it was determined that the Packard engine was less suitable for this application than other available commercial engines, so the Ford 368 UC engine was adopted at an early development stage.

Other problems were encountered at this time. Cooling difficulties were experienced with the water-cooled Ford engine which required increased engine compartment cooling capacity. On the other hand the air-cooled Continental engine did not perform as well as expected. The 12in. track originally developed for the vehicle exhibited limited durability.

After trials it was found that the aluminium hull construction gave superior ballistic protection

An M106A1 107mm Mortar Carrier named GUARDIAN ANGEL prepares for a fire mission. In the present tactical context, the M106 fires predominantly smoke and illuminating rounds. On the hull side is the base plate and ground mount for the M30 mortar. (Pierre Touzin)

An M113A1 APC with M220 TOW launcher of the Canadian Forces in Germany halts during a tactical exercise, September 1979. The mounting of the Tube-launched Optically-tracked Wire-guided (TOW) missile atop carriers in this manner exposes the gunner throughout the firing sequence. For this reason, TOW carriers have been superseded by the M901 ITV in the US Army. Note the subdued maple leaf marking on the forward hull side, the wire cutter at the front, and the folding M2HB Browning mount. (Pierre Touzin)

and was the most durable and cost effective from a manufacturing standpoint. As a result of the lessons learned from the first group of prototypes, FMC developed two new types of prototypes in late 1957, which were designated T113E1 and T113E2. These were described as 'austerity' vehicles because in addition to correcting the shortcomings found in the previous prototypes, they were designed to keep cost to an absolute minimum. To accomplish this, a decision was taken to adopt less expensive commercially available engines and transmissions which were in large scale production and would be available in the future. The Chrysler A710B (75M in its militarised form) was chosen because it offered the desired performance with suitable cooling characteristics and would be in production for years to come. The Allison TX-200 transmission was adopted since it was readily available and had performed well in the truck industry. The only new assembly to be developed was the controlled

differential, and this was believed to be of minimal risk since most of the components in this design were modelled after a larger but similar unit that was used in the M59 APC.

Although there was a maximum weight limitation for the T113, two different hulls were developed which looked identical externally but differed in armour thickness and overall weight. The purpose of building them was to determine, through testing, data on performance and durability so that the Army could make a final decision on hull configuration based on actual test results. For these prototypes, a wider 15in. track was developed to improve both reliability and performance over the original 12in. type.

Four T113E1 and four T113E2 vehicles and a ballistic hull of each were produced. After successful testing, the heavier T113E2 was selected for production as the basis for the M113 Armored Personnel Carrier. Three pre-production pilots of the final design for the M113 were constructed and tested in 1959 to prove production tooling and manufacturing techniques. The first production M113 APC rolled off the FMC assembly lines at San Jose, California in June 1960, only three years and eight months after the award of the initial development contract. The first US Army order was for 900 vehicles.

Technical Description

Carrier, Personnel, Full-Tracked, Armored, M113:

The M113 Armored Personnel Carrier is a fully tracked vehicle designed to transport a squad of infantry and their equipment. The engine is located at the front of the vehicle to the right of the driver. Alongside the engine and connected to it by a transfer case is an automatic hydro-kinetic torque converter transmission facing rearwards. It is coupled through a universally jointed shaft to the steering mechanism located in front of the engine, from which power is transmitted to the final drive gears and sprockets at the front of the vehicle.

The M113 is powered by a Chrysler V-8 75M water-cooled gasoline engine developing 209bhp at 4,000rpm. After production was initiated, FMC was requested to develop a diesel engine configuration that could be adapted to the production M113 engine compartment. This would provide increased performance, greater fuel economy, and would meet the Army requirement for standardisation on one type of fuel for heavy military vehicles.

The government contract required that FMC design and build prototype vehicles using the Detroit Diesel 6V53 diesel engine. Since it weighed considerably more than the gasoline engine it replaced, the government directed the use of the Allison XTG-90 transmission which was lighter than the M113 power train. However, after intensive study FMC proposed that a power train utilising the M113-type steering differential with the TX100 commercial transmission would be more reliable and less expensive than the Ordnance type XTG-90.

The government held firm to its position that the XTG-90 was the only acceptable approach, and directed that prototypes be built to that configuration. FMC, on the other hand, felt so strongly that the commercial TX100 was the best solution that FMC supplied, at its own expense, a prototype vehicle utilising the FMC-suggested power train for government testing. Comparative

One important derivative of the M113 that has not been adopted by the US Army is the Fitter's Vehicle, which is designed to undertake light repairs and component changes in the field by means of its H1AB hydraulic crane and winch. The Fitter's Vehicle is in service with several armies, notably Israel and Australia. JOY LORRAINE, a 'Fitter's Track' of C Squadron, 1st Armoured Regiment, RAAC, replaces the auxiliary charging set engine of a Centurion Mark 5/1 (AUST) in Phuoc Tuy Province, South Vietnam, 1968. (Peter de Jong)

An M806A1 Armoured Recovery Vehicle (Light) of the Technical Support Troop, 1/15 Royal New South Wales Lancers passes the review stand during the parade to mark the Silver Jubilee of HM Queen Elizabeth II in Sydney, 3 October 1977. (Paul Handel)

tests soon demonstrated that there were serious technical problems with the XTG-90 transmission that would require extensive reworking. Based on the results of the tests and an economic analysis that showed the latter to be far more expensive, the US Army Staff selected the FMC proposal, thus saving the US government millions of dollars. The diesel-powered vehicle designated M113A1 entered production in 1964.

The 6V53 water-cooled two-stroke compression-ignition engine is one of a series based on a common cylinder size produced by the Detroit Diesel Engine Division of the General Motors Corporation, and develops 215bhp at 2,800rpm. Both the gasoline and diesel engines are readily accessible via a large hinged door in the front hull plate behind the trim vane. The top cover may also be raised, allowing easy removal of the whole engine-transmission assembly.

The two engines demand somewhat different transmissions which are of the 'Torqmatic' heavy-duty truck type produced by the Allison Division of GMC. The M113 is fitted with the Allison TX200-2A transmission. This consists of a single-stage torque converter and an epicyclic gearbox giving six forward speeds and one reverse. The driver of the vehicle does not, however, select individual gears but is provided with a shift lever which enables him to select reverse, neutral or one of four ranges of forward gear ratios. The four ranges cover respectively the first and second gears, third and fourth gears, third, fourth and fifth gears and third, fourth, fifth and sixth gears; the 1-2 range

would normally be used for climbing steep grades and the 3-4-5-6 for normal driving. Up and down gear changes within each range are automatic; they are determined by engine speed and accelerator pedal position, making the vehicle easy to drive even in rough terrain.

The M113A1 is fitted with the Allison TX100-1 transmission, which is basically similar but has only three forward speeds giving, nevertheless, four ranges of forward gears: 1, 1-2, 1-2-3, and 2-3. In both systems the hydro-kinetic torque converter is automatically locked up at certain engine speeds by means of a clutch.

The steering mechanism, which is manufactured by FMC, is the same on all vehicles of the M113 series. Designated Model DS200, it is of the Cletrac single-speed geared-differential type with band brakes. The band brakes are connected mechanically to steering levers in the driver's compartment and are used not only to steer the vehicle but also for braking. On the M113A1 each differential output half-shaft has attached to it a brake disc; the associated brake calipers being connected hydraulically to short levers in the driver's compartment. The disc brakes are intended for manoeuvring in confined spaces and they also improve the response of the vehicle when afloat.

From the steering mechanism the drive is taken to final drive units, on either side of the vehicle, and then on to the double track drive sprockets and so to the tracks.

The tracks have a pitch of six inches and are 15in. wide. Their shoes are rubber-backed with removable rubber road pads and are joined by single rubber-bushed pins, providing good road-holding and reduced noise levels. Because the road wheels are sprung by transversely located torsion bars and have to be staggered on one side of the vehicle in relation to the other, the two tracks are of slightly different length: the right-hand track consists of 64 shoes but the left has 63.

There are five dual road wheels on each side. They have a diameter of 24in. and consist of aluminium discs with solid rubber tyres $2\frac{1}{8}$in. wide. Each wheel is located by means of a trailing arm and sprung by a single torsion bar. The front and rear road wheel arms are fitted with hydraulic dampers. Hydraulically operated track adjusters are connected to the idlers to maintain track tension. Track life commonly exceeds the 3,000-mile specification originally laid down and on occasions has even attained 9,000.

The all-welded hull of the M113 is made of an alloy (type 5083) containing, in addition to aluminium, manganese and magnesium, which is produced by cold rolling. Armour thickness varies from $\frac{3}{4}$in. to a maximum of $1\frac{1}{4}$in., providing protection to the occupants from shell fragments and small-arms fire. The driver sits in the front left-hand corner of the vehicle and has a single-piece hatch with four periscopes which opens to the rear. The commander is situated in the centre of the vehicle and has a simple cupola fitted with five episcopes. Behind the commander's position is the cargo hatch above the troop compartment. Ten infantrymen ride in the rear of the vehicle on benches facing inwards. If personnel are not carried the seats can be folded, giving 231 cubic feet of cargo space. There is a hydraulic ramp at the rear incorporating a separate door and operated by the driver.

The M113 is fully amphibious without preparation beyond the raising of the trim vane at the front to stabilise the vehicle during operation in water. The M113 is propelled in water by its tracks at a speed of approximately 3mph. The rubber track shroud on each side of the hull enhances performance in water. Two electric bilge pumps are fitted to discharge water shipped whilst wading, one at the left front and the other at right rear.

The standard armament of the M113 is a flexible .50cal. M2HB Browning mounted at the commander's cupola. The weapon is belt-fed from boxes of 100 rounds and has an elevation of $+53°$, a depression of $-21°$ and 360° of traverse.

ACAV

(Armored Cavalry Assault Vehicle)

The M113 first saw combat in 1962 with the Army of the Republic of Vietnam (ARVN). In March of that year a consignment of 32 M113 APCs destined for Europe was diverted to South Vietnam to aid the hard-pressed ARVN forces against the Communist insurgency.

Two mechanised companies, each with 15 APCs, were organised and they began operations against the Vietcong in the Mekong Delta during June. After some initial problems in developing the most effective means for their employment, the

Gunners of the Royal Artillery prepare an MGM52C Lance missile for firing from an M752 — the launcher vehicle of the M667 Lance Missile Carrier system. (Simon Dunstan)

APCs proved highly successful. The bald statistics representing the number of VC killed and captured were considerable, and the psychological shock effect of the M113 in areas where the ARVN had not previously operated was clearly significant.

Operational experience soon showed, however, that it was not practical to dismount the infantry from an APC until VC positions had been completely overrun. Once the troops dismounted in the water-covered rice paddies much of their advantage in mobility over the VC was lost, whereas the M113 was capable of a sustained speed of 20kph across such terrain.

By these means, constant pressure could be maintained against retreating VC forces, while the .50cal. machine gun was employed to engage and hold the enemy at long range to deter retaliation from RPG teams. To ensure an uninterrupted flow of fire, the gunner dropped the free end of the ammunition belt through his cupola while the first box was being fired. Down below a crew member linked on a new belt and fed it up to the gun. This permitted the gunner to fire without having to change ammunition boxes and reload after every 100 rounds.

Meanwhile other crew members generated further firepower from the open troop compartment hatch, while keeping constant vigil for VC attempting to hide in the water by using hollow reeds as breathing tubes. Any who were spotted were either killed by grenades or crushed in place by the M113s.

Such employment, which was contrary to the contemporary doctrine that emphasised the APC as a means of transporting infantry to the battlefield, met with disfavour among the upper echelons of MACV (Military Assistance Command Vietnam); but despite their protests, the concept

A YPR-765 (Armored Infantry Fighting Vehicle) of the Netherlands Army with 25mm Oerlikon KBA cannon and spaced laminate armour on hull and turret sides, rear hull and lower front hull—the combination of these features provides a considerable increase in firepower and protection over the standard M113A1 APC, while enjoying a high degree of commonality with the latter for ease of logistical support. (Royal Netherlands Army)

of mounted combat became widespread and was readily adopted by American units when they arrived 'in-country'.

The mobility conferred by the M113 to government forces in formerly inaccessible areas of the Mekong Delta and elsewhere was dramatic, although terrain trafficability remained a constant problem. Certain areas did not lend themselves to M113 operations, such as sugar cane and coconut plantations or areas close to rivers and canal banks. The latter type of terrain contained soft, glutinous mud which would not support an M113, causing it to flounder. Rice fields which did not contain water in the rainy season indicated that the foundation was very soft and thus to be avoided. In the dry season, although trafficability was better across rice fields, the overall speed was reduced by the time taken to traverse sun-hardened dikes which, at times, could only be negotiated through the use of explosive charges or ramps. The same dikes could be crushed during the rainy season without losing momentum. Momentum was the key factor in maintaining M113 movement across swampland or flooded rice paddies, as any involuntary halts could result in floundering. As French armour personnel had learned many years before, water buffalo were a good indicator of terrain trafficability. Generally, those areas where the water buffalo eat were safe for M113 movement, but where buffaloes sank to their bellies the terrain was too soft for the M113.

In this way the cross-country mobility of the M113 APC and the paucity of enemy anti-tank weapons made it possible to employ the APC as a fighting vehicle. American units rapidly developed the concept, and to improve fighting capabilities M113 APCs were fitted with a variety of devices, including gunshields for the .50cal. machine guns, side-mounted M60 machine guns, and sandbags or other improvised armour arranged as parapets around the troop compartment so that infantry could fire over the sides.

Such modifications were haphazard at first and entirely dependent on individual units; but when 11th Armored Cavalry Regiment arrived in 1966, the largest US armour formation to be deployed to Vietnam, its M113s were fitted with an armament sub-system devised by FMC. The 'A' model or kit comprised a gunshield for the .50cal. Browning

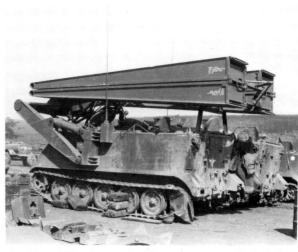

To aid mobility in crossing the many steep-sided ditches, gullies and watercourses in Vietnam, US Army Engineers devised a hydraulically-operated scissors bridge mounted on an M113A1 APC in 1967. The bridge can be unfolded in two minutes without exposure of the two-man crew, and provides a gap crossing capability of 33ft. for a 15-ton vehicle. This M113A1 Marginal Terrain Assault Bridge served with 11th Armored Cavalry Regiment at Phouc Loi in 1969. (John Graber)

and hatch armour around the commander's position providing all-round protection, and two side-mounted M60 machine guns also with gunshields. In this configuration the M113 was designated Armored Cavalry Assault Vehicle or ACAV, a term originated by Lt.Col. Martin D. Howell, commander of 1st Squadron, 11 ACR. A 'B' model or kit, consisting of hatch armour and gunshield for the commander's .50cal. Browning only, was used by mortar carriers.

Many M113 APCs in mechanised infantry units were also modified with 'A' or 'B' kits and, although they were all intents and purposes identical to ACAVs and were often employed in the same role, the term ACAV was only correctly applied to those vehicles used by cavalry units.

The ACAV itself underwent many modifications. All seats except the driver's were removed to make room for ammunition cans stacked in two-deep layers, wall-to-wall on the floor of the troop compartment. Together with crew kit bags, water jerrycans, cartons of combat rations, the essential beer cooler, spare gun barrels, M79 grenade launchers and ammunition, crew weapons, boxes of demolition charges and hand grenades, hammocks, tool box and tow cables, this stowage meant that space was at a premium.

Track shrouds were removed to prevent the build-up of mud and debris underneath. In most units the floor of the driver's and troop compartments was laid with sandbags to reduce mine damage and personnel casualties. To minimise further the threat of mines, ACAVs were fitted with 'belly armor' of titanium plates beneath the hull and sponsons.

The M113 and the associated ACAV proved to be the most effective armoured fighting vehicle of the Vietnam War. The M113 was in the forefront of innumerable battles in that vicious conflict, as this account by William Kestell, a veteran of 4/23rd Infantry (Mechanized), 25th Infantry Division, relates:

Infantrymen of 25th Infantry Division scan the treeline as an M113A1 APC of 2nd Battalion, 22nd Infantry (Mechanized) forges through dense undergrowth in the Dog's Head area during the incursion into Cambodia, June 1970. Note the bumper number 'B13' is repeated on a strip down the rear hull side. (Armor Magazine)

A graphic illustration of mounted combat: ACAVs of 'The Blackhorse Regiment' deploy in 'herringbone formation' during a search-and-clear mission in Vietnam, 1967. This tactic allowed a great volume of fire to be delivered to either roadside in order to counter ambushes. (Armor Magazine)

'On the morning of 25 March 1968—the day before my 23rd birthday—I found myself on Highway 1 on a road-clearing operation with 2nd Section, Recon Platoon, HHC 4/23rd Infantry (Mechanized) of the 25th Division. We were heading out from Cu Chi, north to Trang Bang. It was our turn as point vehicle, but that was nothing to get excited about. Other operations like this had been milk runs. We'd get to Trang Bang before 1200 hours, and would lay over there until recalled to Cu Chi, or until a convoy came along, in which case we'd join it for the run up to Tay Ninh.

'I had arrived in Vietnam in January and was first assigned as an M60 gunner on No. 38, "The Ugly American".[1] Jeff, her regular driver, was due for R&R so, after a few weeks, he began breaking me in as relief driver. I liked being a gunner, but I knew I'd be a driver until a better assignment came along; besides, I wouldn't have to walk so much. When Jeff got back I was transferred to No. 33, "Mellow Yellow".

[1]See colour plate B1.

An M132A1 Flamethrower of 1st Squadron, 11 ACR, fords a stream during Operation 'Atlas Wedge', 1969. The M132 was an M113 APC fitted with a cupola mounting an M10-8 flame gun and co-axial M73 machine gun—this vehicle, BURN BABY BURN, has a supplementary M2HB Browning on the cupola roof. (Tim Page)

"Mellow" was an old M113A1 armored personnel carrier, and nobody knew how she got her name. It wasn't what I would have called her, but I thought it was bad luck to change a name. It just isn't done. She had all sorts of little quirks, like spraying diesel fuel into the driver's compartment and using a couple of gallons of water a day. Maintenance had given up trying to find the leak. We had just given her new suspension, road wheels, drive and idler sprockets, so she would now do 50-plus without a fuss. I simply got used to the little things and planned around them.

'Our section that day consisted of four APCs, each with a crew of four: TC (track commander), driver, M60 gunner and rifleman. Old No. 33 and one of the other APCs had replaced the rifleman with a 90mm recoilless for added punch. A detachment of engineers operated with us, bringing an articulated scraper and a couple of dump trucks full of gravel to fill in any road damage we might find. We were 19 men in all.

'We were about a mile or two south of Trang Bang when a call came over the radio. An American infantry company had come upon an enemy force of unknown size, and was chasing it. Our section leader made a fast check and found that we were in a perfect position to act as a blocking force when they broke from the woodline about 300-plus metres away. Between the jungle and the road was nothing but open paddy area, a beautiful killing zone with little or no cover. When the NVA hit that paddy, it would be a slaughter.

'With four .50cals., four M60s, four M79s, two 90mms, our riflemen and the engineers, we could

EVE OF DESTRUCTION **an ACAV of 1st Squadron, 11ACR negotiates an Armored Vehicle Launched Bridge (AVLB) during a search-and-destroy mission near the Michelin Rubber Plantation, Vietnam, 1969. The FMC ACAV kit comprises a gunshield for the .50cal. Browning; hatch armour known as 'the bathtub' surrounding the commander; and gunshields for the side-mounted M60 machine guns. The second ACAV has floatation cells fitted to the trim vane and hull front to compensate for the extra weight of the 'belly armor' which was added to M113 APCs and ACAVs in Vietnam from 1969 as increased protection against mines. (Tim Page)**

easily blunt any movement across that stretch of ground. We got the order to halt, and the drivers pivoted the APCs 45 degrees right to a head-on position toward the expected enemy breakout point. Everyone except TCs and drivers dismounted and took up positions in the ditch in front of the vehicles.

'Larry, who was M60 gunner, took two boxes of ammo with him, and we tossed over three or four more just for good measure, giving him about 1,000 rounds. Lloyd had plenty of rounds for his 90mm—about 12 to 15 of HE [high explosive] and Beehive mixed. The excitement mounted.

'I went aft and brought up a few more boxes of .50cal. so it would be handy, positioned my M79 and my ready rounds, and got in position as Dave swung the .50 out toward the jungle. All we could do now was wait.

'At the edge of the woodline! Everyone tensed.

'Then someone shouted, "Wait! Hold it! They're ARVNs!" It was a squad-sized unit, maybe a bit larger, moving out of the woodline, heading south-west. They were probably running

An infantry squad form a 'skirmishing line' after dismounting from an M113 following the doctrine for which the M113 APC was designed, whereby infantry assault an objective on foot, having been transported to the battlefield by APC. The M113 entered service with the US Army in 1960 and will continue to serve into the 1990s. (US Army SC587504)

ahead of the enemy, frequently the case with ARVNs. We waited and held our fire.

'There they are. NVA! The .50s on all four APCs let go almost in one voice, but you could tell each TC by his special "signature", like a wireless operator. Howie on No. 38 fired his usual short-spaced, two-round bursts; Dave favored three-round groups. The 60s joined in, firing long bursts. I heard Lloyd fire, laying an HE round at the edge of the woodline.

'I saw more and more NVA break out and I began putting out HE rounds. I fired only a couple before I noticed that Dave had nearly gone through the first box of rounds. I got another box ready to go. We had practiced doing this fast so, just as he was running the last rounds through the gun, I had the next box ready. The feed cover went up as I tossed the empty box over the front end and slammed the full one onto the tray. Dave grabbed the pig-tail of ammo which was hanging out and laid it in the receiver. Then he slammed down the feed cover with his left hand and yanked the charger with the other in a nearly simultaneous motion, and the gun let loose again.

'Streams of tracers poured from every weapon on line. The fire was withering, but still the NVA came out of the jungle. We killed them, but more took their place. There was a sea of NVA, and I found it didn't pay to aim. Just load, point, shoot. Load, point, shoot! I put out round after round. I stopped to reload Dave and then went back into action. I was going through rounds so fast that the barrel was getting hot; at this rate, my ready supply would soon be exhausted.

'Bang! I felt a close concussion, and Dave rocketed out from behind the gun. What the hell? The ammo box sizzled and rounds cooked off! I looked at my left knee. I'm hit! It didn't hurt— it was more a warm, glowing sensation like a fire. A fire?

'From down in the ditch, one of the medics yelled up, asking if I'd been hit too. Hit too? Dave. Damn straight, I'm hit! But I knew he wasn't going to come up to fix it. Well, I thought, if we are burning, I'm not going to stay up here with several thousand rounds of .50cal. and 7.62mm down below.

'I grabbed the M79, tossed it over the side and bailed out over the rear. Opening the small rear door, I went in to get the wooden 90mm packing case in which I carried my hoard of M79 rounds.

With its trim vane raised, this M113A1 APC displays the gaudy four-colour camouflage scheme, extending to the crewmen's helmets, adopted by US 7th Army in Europe during the 1970s. The M113 APC has no nickname in US service beyond 'PC' or 'Poppa Charlie'. (MoD)

I had been saving these for the last few weeks, ever since we had been put on allocations after our ammo dump went up during a rocket attack.

'I tossed the case out the door, jumped out and dogged the door behind me. Whop! An RPG tore into No. 33. If I had been inside I could have said goodbye. I dropped prone. Where in the hell is that damn M79? I had been disoriented when I tossed it over the side—I found it directly in the line of fire, about six feet from the vehicle. I slithered out on my belly, got it and retreated to what little cover the tracks afforded. At least I wasn't out in the open and I had an unrestricted field of fire.

'Suddenly, the asphalt road in front of me exploded in a shower of fragments—and I couldn't see! Chunks of asphalt cut my face, and my lip was puffed up and bleeding. I scrunched back a little

farther behind the tracks and finally managed to focus. If the NVA on the other end of that AK had used just a fraction more elevation, he'd have hit me.

'The NVA numbers grew, despite the intensity of our fire. Point, shoot. Get those rounds out.

'Whop! Another RPG hit No. 33. She wouldn't need the $2\frac{1}{2}$ pages of parts and equipment to get her ready to pass inspection. I'd joked about losing the paperwork, since she probably would be junk before the stuff arrived. Suddenly the joke no longer seemed funny. One of the other APCs had been hit too, and was burning. RPGs flew behind us, in front as they fell short, and heavily to my right, all up and down the line. Both dump trucks had been hit and their gravel was strewn all over the road.

'I heard the snap, snap of incoming overhead. Off to my right front, a head popped up every so often from behind a wall attached to a small hootch. I aimed and waited for the head to reappear. Poomp, Crash. Shit! Too high! I

reloaded feverishly. The second round hit just below the lip, tearing out a big chunk of wall and part of the roof.

'I blindly reached for another round. But now I had to feel around for the dwindling supply. I tried to pace my rate of fire, but then decided to shoot them all now, while the NVA were still far enough out for the warhead to arm. The remaining rounds went in no time, except for two spares in my right trouser pocket—just in case!

'Just then I saw him, an NVA making a run from the hootch. I stood up and grabbed an M16 from the vehicle, threw off the safety to full-auto. I emptied the magazine as the NVA vanished in a cloud of dust and lead. I ducked back, peered out a second later and saw nothing but a bundle of rags which moments before had been an enemy soldier.

'The three of us made our way south to join the rest of our dismounted troops. Our section leader told us to get to the far side of the road and head north toward Trang Bang. As I crawled up the bank, my knee hurt—and worse, it was stiff and would not bend. That meant that all I'd be able to do was walk across that open road. It would be

Besides its combat use in numerous conflicts of the past 20 years, the M113 has been widely employed by contingencies of the United Nations for peace-keeping duties. Bearing prominent marking panels, Canadian M113 APCs of the UN Peace Keeping Force in Cyprus (UNFICYP) patrol a road near Nicosia, August 1974. (UN)

Sometimes referred to as the 'M113½', the M113 Command and Reconnaissance (C&R) vehicle was developed in 1966 by FMC, utilising many components of the M113 APC, as an agile scout vehicle with superior mobility to wheeled vehicles. The C&R was adopted by the Netherlands Army and, in 1968, by the Canadian Army with some design changes under the designation Lynx. Here, a Lynx of the Canadian Forces in Germany conducts a reconnaissance mission. (Canadian Forces Photo)

Typical of the extravagant markings applied to some AFVs in Vietnam is this M113A1 APC of 4/23rd Infantry (Mechanized) as it prepares to move out from Fire Support Base Lynch near Xuan Loc, November 1970. Above the title YOU ONLY LIVE TWICE is the name DAY TRIPPER in 1960s psychedelic lettering, while behind and also below the vehicle registration numbers are stylised tomahawks—referring to the nickname of 4/23rd Mech. (US Army SC659825)

suicide. Larry and Lloyd broke and ran across. They made it.

'I stretched myself out and started rolling across. I stopped for just a second when I saw one of the engineers break from the ditch. He ran halfway across the road and turned toward the NVA. His M16 was dirty, so he had to cock it manually. He did this, fired once, and was cocking it again when a burst caught him. He spun around and hit the road, screaming and writhing in agony. It was horrible, but lasted only a few seconds. He lay still. I rolled even faster and reached the ditch almost immediately. We regrouped and started to get organized. Now was no time to panic.

'Number 38 and the other functioning APC prepared to pull out and all the troops who could scrambled aboard. We were too far away, and there was simply no more room. Jeff threw her into gear, and tromped the accelerator. She leaped forward, the other following closely.

'I remember looking up at "The Ugly American" as she tore by us. I could see my friends aboard and the looks on Jeff, Howie, T. J., Jack, Arty and

Doc's faces. There was no question of their stopping or even slowing for us. A sitting target could be hit many times in the space of a few seconds. I knew they hated to leave us. But our unit was going to be overrun and those who could live to fight another time would be foolish to throw their lives away on a gallant but hollow gesture. The engine sound faded as they escaped, RPGs following them.'

Grievously wounded in the legs—an enemy round set off the propellant of the M79 rounds which he describes keeping in his pocket in the account above—Kestell was to lie alone on the sun-scorched battlefield throughout that day. He survived being looted by NVA soldiers, and being strafed by Allied gunships and bombarded by artillery, before he was eventually rescued at nightfall.

Major Production Variants

Since it first entered service with the US Army in 1960, the M113 has been produced in larger quantities than any other American armoured vehicle. By 1964, 10,000 vehicles of the M113 family had been produced. In 1970 the number reached 40,000 and today the total stands at over

70,000, including 4,000 built by Oto Melara for the Italian Army and for export. Manufacture continues with no abatement of orders.

Production on such a vast scale leads to a low unit cost, which in turn makes possible availability in greater numbers within a given budget. At one time the M113 cost as little as $22,000. Despite the ravages of inflation, the current cost is approximately $100,000, which in real terms represents virtually no increase. Obviously, the actual cost depends on many factors such as model, volume of order and individual requirements of the customer. The low procurement and maintenance costs have attracted many buyers, and the M113 is in service with the armies of over 50 nations.

The versatile M113 has spawned a whole host of special purpose variants based on the standard chassis. The wide variety of applications has led to scores of vehicles, both proposed and actually manufactured. Besides these, there have been numerous modifications in foreign service. Many of them are of a minor nature related to changes in armament or fittings. If these are included, the total number of variants in the M113 Family of Vehicles (FOV) runs into three figures; but only

An M577 of Battery B, 3rd Battalion, 18th Artillery, enters Camp Radcliff after operations in the field in support of 1st Cavalry Division in Vietnam, August 1966. The letters IFFV denote 1st Field Force Vietnam ('Eye Force Vee' when spoken), while above is the vehicle weight classification. Markings on the hull side are the divisional patch of First Cavalry with a diminutive 1st Field Force insignia beside it, and the commonplace Playboy Bunny emblem beyond the national white star. (US Army SC632931)

An M548 Cargo Carrier of Battery B, 5th Battalion, 4th Artillery, of 1st Brigade, 5th Infantry Division (Mechanized), transports ammunition to Fire Support Base Holcomb in Vietnam, July 1970. The M548 proved invaluable for logistical support over the marginal roads and hostile terrain of Vietnam. The M548 can carry a six-ton payload, and the front-mounted winch enables the carrier to recover itself from soft terrain or ditches. (US Army SC657309)

the principal systems that have been used operationally or are about to enter widespread service are described and illustrated here.

Throughout its life, FMC has continually improved the M113 series to keep abreast of technological and tactical innovations. As a result, the loaded weight of the M113 has risen from the original 11.75 tons and has reached 14 tons in the M548. The decreasing power-to-weight ratios have lessened performance, and reliability is lower due to the greater strain on major components.

In consequence, FMC has introduced a series of improvements, many of which derive from the development cycle of the AIFV. The M113A1 Modernization Program is divided into three aspects. The first is designated as the Suspension and Cooling Product Improvement Program (PIP), the second as the Improved Power PIP and the third as the Extended Vehicle Program. The first two aim at improving RAM-D (Reliability, Availability, Maintainability and Durability), while the Extended Vehicle Program will provide new capabilities for greater loads on both M113A1 and M548.

The Suspension and Cooling PIP applies to the standard M113A1 and incorporates a revised

Unlike the majority of its contemporaries, the M113 is fully amphibious without preparation—an attribute that proved itself in full during the Vietnam War. M113s of the 7th Mechanized Rifle Company, one of the first two ARVN units to be equipped with the vehicle, train for waterborne operations prior to deployment in the Mekong Delta, 1962. (USIS)

cooling system with the position of the fan and the radiator reversed, allowing the vehicle to operate at higher ambient temperatures without over-heating, and also extending engine life. The improved suspension provides a smoother cross-country ride and an increase in speed of about 3mph by means of high-strength torsion bars, greater roadwheel travel, and an extra set of shock absorbers at the second roadwheel station to control vehicle pitch. These features were introduced into the production line in July 1979, and vehicles so fitted are classified as the M113A2.

Various options are available for the M113A2 including a dual air source heater which allows employment of a collective CBR system; and external, rear-mounted fuel tanks which reduce the chance of secondary fires when hit and increase interior hull space by 20 per cent. The US Army has not adopted these fuel tanks in series but several foreign customers have, including Israel (see colour plate G2).

The weight of the M113A1 APC is 24,600lbs. Other members of the M113A1 family such as the M106A1, the M730 and M548 have reached combat loaded weights of 26,450, 27,775 and 28,400lbs respectively. All the vehicles possess the same power plant, and power-to-weight ratios

range from 17.1 HP/ton for the M113A1 APC to as low as 14.8 HP/ton for the M730. Weights of other M113A1 vehicles have also increased disproportionately due to the incorporation of heavier weapon systems, such as the Improved TOW Vehicle. Increasing vehicle weights require an increase in engine power to retain performance characteristics and reliability.

This has been achieved through the Improved Power PIP by replacing the GMC 6V53 (210bhp) diesel with the turbo-charged version, 6V53-T (275bhp). The present power train is replaced by the X290-3 Detroit Diesel Allison transmission which incorporates hydrostatic steering to provide smoother turning and reduced shock load on the suspension, while its greater efficiency results in more horsepower at the sprocket, and fuel savings. The driver's controls have also been changed, and the conventional steering levers have been replaced by a steering wheel and foot brake. Vehicles with these features, together with those of the A2 model, are classified M113A3.

Further improvements are being investigated for the M113 FOV. These include a high-output heavy-duty electrical system, a ballistic liner inside the vehicles to ameliorate the effects of shaped charge attack, a fire suppression system to enhance crew survival, new night sights and CBR protection among others.

The Extended Vehicle Program relates to experimental models of the M113A1 and M548 with longer hulls and one additional set of road wheels to allow more cargo or troops to be carried. These 'stretched' versions are designated M113A1-S and M548A1E1.

M48 Chaparral Forward Area Air-Defense Missile System

The Chaparral is an adaptation of the successful US Navy Sidewinder 1C air-to-air infra-red homing missile to a mobile surface-to-air weapon system. Chaparral is fired from a four-rail launcher designated M54 mounted on an M730 chassis, a modified version of the M548 Cargo Carrier.

Developed by the Aeronutronic Division of Ford Aerospace and Communications Corporation, the M48 was placed in production in 1966 and entered service with the US Army in 1969. The first missiles (MIM-72) were identical to the Navy version, but an improved model (MIM-72C), featuring an improved proximity fuze and a new high explosive blast-fragmentation warhead over twice the size of the original, entered service in July 1978. A further improved model (MIM-72F) has a smokeless engine to reduce the battlefield signature, and a new guidance system increases resistance against infra-red countermeasures such as high-intensity flares dispensed from aircraft.

The Chaparral was devised as a clear-weather, daylight system whereby the gunner either acquires the target visually, or is informed when targets are approaching by the AN/MPQ-49 FAAR (Forward Area Alerting Radar), since the M48 itself is not equipped with radar. Once the target is detected, the gunner tracks the aircraft in his optical sight until an audible tone in his headset notifies him that the target is within infra-red sensing range. The missile is then launched and its heat-seeking guidance takes over, the proximity fuze assuring detonation even without a direct hit.

The M48 is currently being fitted with a Forward-Looking Infra-red (FLIR) thermal-imaging device to give a night-time capability. The FLIR sight will also improve the system's performance in daylight smoke and haze. The missile has a maximum range of 5,000 metres and a maximum effective altitude of about 2,500 metres.

The M730 Chaparral Missile Carrier has the engine and crew compartment at the front with the M54 missile launch station at the rear. The collapsible crew compartment is folded down and covered by blast plates. The launch station is mounted on an extendable base which is lowered for travelling and raised for firing. The M54 has 360° traverse and the launcher rails an elevation of +90° and depression of −5°. The launching sequence can be operated by a single crewman.

The Chaparral is employed in Air-Defense Battalions in conjunction with the M163 Vulcan. It is expected to remain in service with the US Army into the 1990s. The Israelis have used the Chaparral in combat during the October War of 1973 and in Lebanon.

M106 Armored Self-Propelled 107mm Mortar and M125 Armored Self-Propelled 81mm Mortar

Both the M106 and M125 share the same configuration on a modified M113 vehicle. The hull top has been altered to accommodate a large circular three-piece hatch hinged at the hull sides. The mortars are mounted on the rear hull floor which has been reinforced to absorb recoil shock. The 4.2in. (107mm) M30 mortar of the M106 faces rearwards and fires through an arc of 43° to right of and 46° to left of centre. The 81mm M29 mortar is mounted on a turntable with 360°

Carrying the indispensable RPG screen on the rear hull, an ARVN M113 APC moves forward with the vehicle commander behind the driver (unlike on US APCs and ACAVs, where he manned the .50cal. Browning) and his American adviser beside the gunner. Note the 'belly armor' extending up the lower hull front, and the hull side peppered by small arms fire. (Armor Magazine)

A number of M113 APCs in ARVN service were fitted with machine gun cupolas, such as this Cadillac Gage M74C type mounting twin .30cal. Brownings, to provide greater protection to the gunner. Although effective, these cupolas were not generally adopted as the .50cal. Browning gave greater firepower. There are many machine gun cupolas and enclosed weapon stations currently available for mounting on M113 APCs in order to increase firepower and protection. (US Army SC661438)

traverse. The M106 carries 93 rounds (M106A1, 88 rounds) of ammunition stowed along the hull walls. The M125 carries 114 mortar bombs. The M106A1 and M125A1 diesel-powered versions were produced from 1965.

The M30 mortar fires HE, illuminating and smoke ammunition out to 5,650 metres at a sustained rate of fire of three rounds per minute. The M29 81mm mortar fires HE, illuminating and WP to a range of 4,700 metres at a sustained rate of fire from four to 12 rounds per minute depending on the type of ammunition used.

The US Army has adopted the British L16 81mm mortar (XM252) as a replacement for the M30 and M29. The XM252 has a range of 5,775 metres, matching that of the M30, but has far superior minimum-range performance. The 81mm bomb weighs only one-third as much as the 4.2in. round, but on account of the XM252's high

sustained rate of fire of 15 rounds per minute, the total weight of a timed bombardment is almost as great as for the M30. Both the M106A1 and M125A1 will be re-armed in due course, by which time the mortar carriers will incorporate the improvements of the M113A2. Other users of the M106 have modified their mortar carriers to accept 120mm mortars in place of the M30. Germany has modified her vehicles to accept a Tampella mortar, Switzerland the M64, Israel the Soltam and Italy a Thomson-Brandt weapon.

M132 Self-Propelled Flame Thrower

The M132 is a modified M113 APC with the commander's cupola replaced by an M10-8 flame gun and 200 gallons of fuel stored in the troop compartment. The flame gun has an effective range of 150 yards and sufficient fuel for 30 seconds of firing. Production of the M132 was undertaken by FMC at Charleston, West Virginia: 201 M132 vehicles and 150 of the diesel-powered M132A1 type were built before production ceased in 1965.

Prior to this, M10-8 flame thrower kits had been despatched to Vietnam in 1962 for fitting to existing M113 APCs. M132s were widely used by both US and ARVN forces in Vietnam, where they were nicknamed 'Zippos'. Flame thrower units were supported by an armoured version of the M548, the XM45E1, acting as a service vehicle for fuel replenishment. The M132 is no longer in active service with the US Army.

M163A1 20mm Vulcan Air-Defense Gun

The companion of Chaparral in the US Army's composite divisional Air-Defense Battalions, the Vulcan is a revolving six-barrelled gun mounted on a derivative of the M113 APC, designated M741.

Under the auspices of the Aircraft Equipment Division of the General Electric Company, development of the Vulcan Air Defense System (VADS) began in 1964 involving a self-propelled version (M163) and a towed model (M167) mounted on a single-axle M42 carriage for air-borne and airmobile operations. Trials of the tracked system were conducted in 1965 and production began in 1967. The M163 was accepted into service in August 1968, and later in the same year a test platoon of six vehicles was despatched to Vietnam for combat trials; they were used mainly for convoy escort in the absence of an enemy air threat.

Vulcan is a fair-weather daylight system. The fire control system consists of a Range-Only Radar that can track targets out to 5,000 yards, and a lead-computing gunsight with which the gunner tracks the target. The radar is slaved to the optical line of sight and supplies target range and range-rate information to the sight generator. With this data, the sight automatically computes the future target position and adds the required super-elevation to engage the target. The tracking time necessary to establish the lead angle is about one second. A green light appears in the sight optics when the radar has acquired the target and the aircraft is within effective range. The gun is then fired.

The M61A1 20mm six-barrelled gun is a derivative of the Gatling gun used on jet aircraft. Two rates of fire are available to the gunner: 1,000 rounds per minute for use in the ground role, and 3,000 rounds per minute against aircraft. Bursts of ten, 30, 60 or 100 rounds can be fired at the higher rate. The vehicle carries 2,100 rounds of ammunition of which 1,030 are ready to fire, the remainder being in reserve inside the hull.

The turret is electrically traversed and elevated. The weapon has 360° traverse with an elevation of +80° and −5° of depression. The maximum effective slant range for air defence is 1,600 metres, partly owing to the self-destruct mechanism of the M246 High Explosive Incendiary Tracer ammunition. Maximum horizontal range in the ground role with the contact-fused M56A3 High Explosive Incendiary rounds is 4,500 metres.

The M741 Vulcan Weapon Chassis is a modified M113 with a suspension lock-out mechanism to provide a stable platform on firing, an additional circular hatch in the roof in place of the standard troop compartment hatch, and floatation cells on the hull sides and trim vane to retain an amphibious capability with the heavier weapon system installed.

The US Army has 379 M163A1s in its inventory (the M163A1 has an upgraded radar); each battalion has 24 M163s (two batteries of 12 guns each) and 24 Chaparral systems (two batteries

each with 12 launchers). The Vulcan has seen combat in Vietnam, with the Moroccan Army against the Polisario Front, and with the Israelis during the 1973 War and in Lebanon in 1982 — when an M163 was credited with shooting down a Syrian MiG aircraft.

M548 Cargo Carrier

The XM548 was designed in 1960 to meet a US Army Signal Corps requirement for a highly mobile transporter to carry assorted equipments such as the AN/MPQ-32 Hostile Artillery Radar System. The vehicle incorporated automotive components of the M113 but proved unsuccessful, so a modified version with a diesel engine, the XM548E1, was developed using the powerpack, suspension and components of the M113A1. Trials of three prototypes were conducted in 1964, and the vehicle was type-classified the following year as the M548 Cargo Carrier. Production began in late 1965 at FMC's plant in Charleston, West Virginia.

The M548 is an unarmoured logistical support vehicle for transporting ammunition and supplies over difficult terrain. The engine and crew

Vietnamese armour personnel were the first to fight mounted from M113 APCs rather than as mechanised infantry to assault positions on foot. Subsequently, gun-shields were added to protect the .50cal. gunners, and .30cal. Brownings were fitted either side of the troop compartment for greater firepower, as on this M113 of ARVN 10th Armoured Cavalry Regiment in Cambodia, May 1970. (US Army SC655817)

compartment are at the front and the full-width cab accommodates four men sitting abreast. The cargo compartment, which can carry a payload of six tons, has a rear opening secured by two watertight doors. The upper door is hinged on the side. The lower door, which mounts the towing pintle, is hinged on the bottom. Forming the cargo deck are six hollow aluminium extruded plates that are bolted in place in either of two positions: the upper position provides a continuous flat bed, while the lower permits carrying more cargo or offers leg room for seated personnel. The cargo area can be enclosed by using a standard vinyl-coated nylon cover-supported by aluminium bows.

The M548 has the same running gear as the M113A1, but, being heavier when loaded, has torsion bars of greater diameter, and the final drives have a different gear ratio. The vehicle is fully amphibious and is propelled in water by its tracks, although this is no longer a requirement in the US Army. An M66 machine gun mount allows either a .50cal. or 7.62mm machine gun to be

fitted over the cab. For handling heavy stores, a 1,500lb-capacity chain hoist and trolley can be mounted on an I-beam attached to the second rear cargo cover bows, allowing loads within three feet of the tailgate to be lifted and positioned anywhere within the cargo area.

The versatile M548 chassis has been adapted for a variety of specialised roles, and derivatives include the M667 Lance Missile Carrier, M727 HAWK Missile Carrier, M730 Chaparral Missile Carrier and the RCM748 Tracked Rapier. Many countries have modified their M548s for other uses, carrying radars, fire control systems, mine dispensers, or as the basis for indigenous anti-aircraft weapons such as the Italian Indigo— MEI Mobile Air Defence System.

The current model of the M548 series is the M548A1 Cargo/System Carrier, incorporating improved cooling and suspension components which give increased engine life, reliability and higher cross-country speeds.

In 1977, FMC developed a stretched version of the M548 with an additional set of wheels to provide greater cargo space or larger area as a weapons station platform. Classified as the M548A1E1, it features a 300bhp turbo-charged engine and a transmission with hydrostatic steering. This version forms the basis of the Swiss Oerlikon GDF-CO3 'David' 35mm SPAA System.

ARVN M113 APCs and an M577 command vehicle of Task Force 255 advance through the Parrot's Beak area of Cambodia during the 1970 incursion. Note the abundance of stowage on these vehicles; the wooden box, carried by so many ARVN APCs and seen here on the top rear quarter of the left-hand M113, contained the crew's food and cooking utensils. (US Army SC655819)

1: M113 APC, 21st Mech. Rifle Co., ARVN 21st Div.; 1962

2: M113 APC, Armor Regt., ROK Capital Div.; 1967

1: M113A1 APC, US 4/23rd Inf.(Mech.), 25th Inf.Div.; 1968

2: M577A1, US 4th Cav., 1st Inf.Div.; 1968

B

STANDING ORDER
FOR
TROOPERS OF THE
11 US CAVALRY
"FIND THE BASTARDS
—THEN PILE ON"

1: M106A1, US 11th Armd.Cav.Regt.; 1969

2: M548, US 168th Eng.Bn.; 1969

C

12 CAR FIFTY-FOUR
22B GOOK CRUSHER
33A GREEN MACHINE

1: M113A1 APC, B Sqn., 3rd Cav.Regt.,RAAC; 1970

2: M113A1(FS), A Sqn., 3rd Cav.Regt., RAAC; 1971

D

1 : ACAV, Troop B, 3rd Sqn., 4th Cav.; 1969

2 : ACAV, Troop E, 2nd Sqn., 11th Armd.Cav.Regt.; 1969

3: ACAV, Troop A, 1st Sqn., 10th Cav.; 1971

E

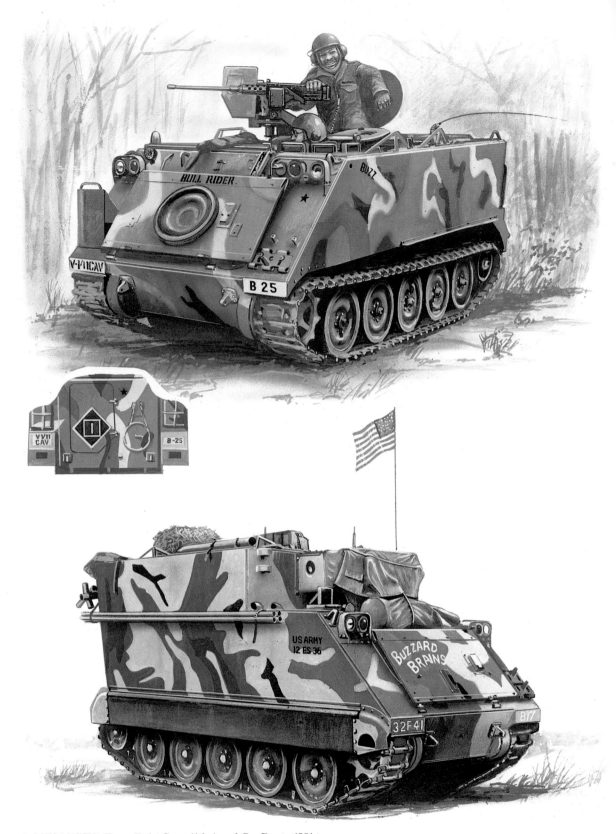

1: M113A1(CSV), Troop B, 1st Sqn., 11th Armd.Cav.Regt.; 1981

2: M577A1 of a Battery Bn., Artillery, US 7th Army; West Germany, 1978

F

1: M113A2 APC, 8th Inf.Regt., Royal Moroccan Army; Sahara, 1979

2: M113A1 'Zelda', Israeli Defence Forces; Lebanon, 1982

G

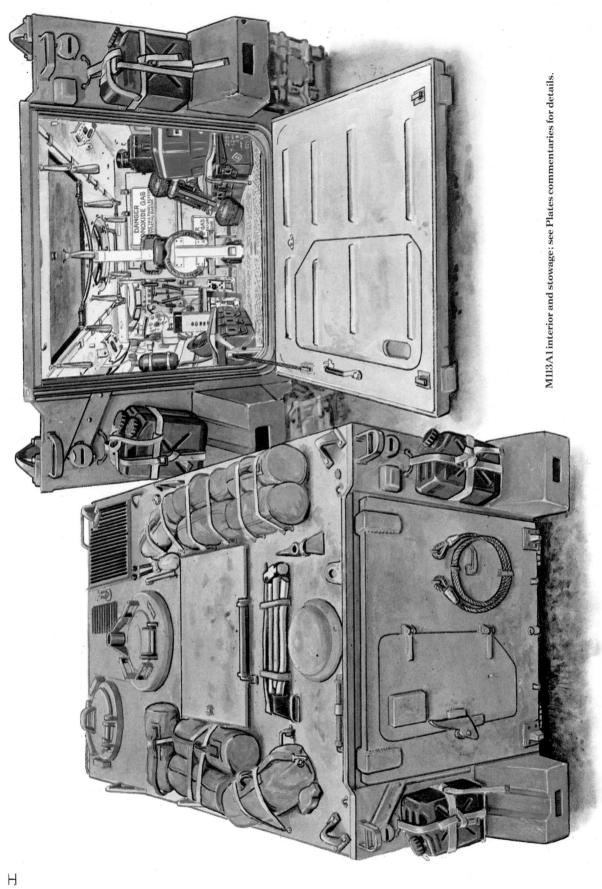

M113A1 interior and stowage; see Plates commentaries for details.

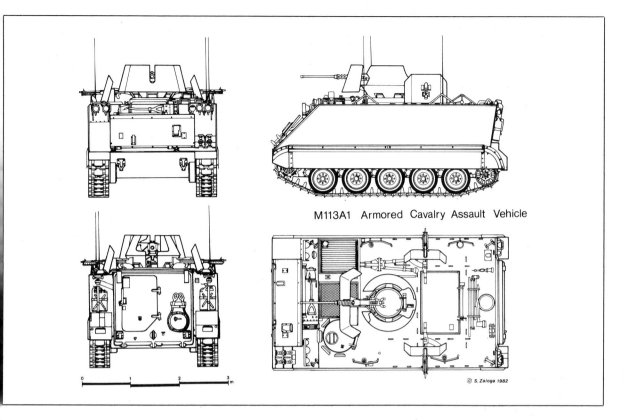

M113A1 Armored Cavalry Assault Vehicle

© S. Zaloga 1982

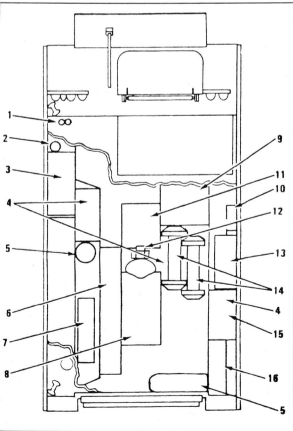

(Above) **1/76th plan of ACAV (Steven Zaloga)**

Internal stowage plan of the cavalry scout version of the M113: (1) Binoculars (2) M11 Decontaminating Apparatus (3) Reel Equipment CE-11, Radiacmeter, Cable Telephone WD-1/TT × 2, Antenna, Telephone Set TA-312/PT, Telescope, Night Vision Goggles AN/PVS-5 × 2 (4) Alice Packs × 5 (5) Duffel Bags × 5 (6) Ammunition Boxes (7) M60 MG Kit strapped to wall (8) Bedrolls × 5, Combat Meals × 2 cases (9) Night Vision Sight AN/PVS-4 (10) Dragon Tracker (11) case Combat Meals, Squad Box for weapon cleaning kit, spares, batteries etc. (12) Radio Set AN/PRC-77 (13) Night Vision Sight AN/TVS-5 (14) Dragon Missile Rounds × 6 (15) Chemical Overgarment, Boots and Gloves × 5 (16) Map Canister.

M577 Carrier, Command Post: Light Tracked

The first few prototypes of an Armored Command Post Vehicle designated XM577 were converted from existing M113 APCs at Detroit Arsenal in early 1962. Production was begun in November by FMC and the vehicle was type-classified as the M577 in March 1963. The first order for 270 vehicles was completed between December 1962 and May 1963. The M577 has been built, off and on, for the US Army and Foreign Military Sales ever since.

The M577 is based on the M113 chassis with an enlarged superstructure providing protection and

The crew of an ARVN M113 APC relax under a sunshade while standing guard on a roadside. The roof is lined with boxes of ammunition for the shielded M2HB Browning and for the tripod-mounted M1919A4 Brownings lashed to the rear hull top. Similar in concept to the ACAV, the vehicle had no designation in ARVN service but was known by crewmen as *cua sat*—'iron crab'. (Armor Magazine)

mobility for field commanders. The top of the hull has been raised two feet to provide full head room for personnel standing erect. The increased volume provides space for maps, radios and related equipment required for command functions.

The standard 85-gallon fuel cell has been replaced by two 60-gallon cells, one on each side of the vehicle, and each cell acts as the foundation for a 90in. table with three folding leaves. The commander's seat and cupola and .50cal. Browning have been eliminated to maintain an amphibious capability. A simple folding platform is substituted at the commander's station.

A 28-volt, 150-ampere (4.2kw) auxiliary generator is mounted on the front vertical hull plate. It may be run in position or used dismounted, to provide power for lighting and radios. A tent extension and poles are carried on the rear of the vehicle, providing a greater working area at the back with provision for operation under black-out conditions. Up to four M577 vehicles

can be connected by these extensions.

As well as being used as a command post, the M577 is employed by artillery fire control units, signal units and as a mobile medical treatment centre. The M557A1 incorporates the changes of the M113A1, and the M577A2 those of the M113A2.

M667 Lance Missile Carrier for MGM52C Lance Battlefield Support Missile

Lance is currently the most powerful missile available to the tactical ground commander for engaging targets beyond the range of cannon artillery. The missile weighs 2,850lbs. and carries either conventional munitions or nuclear warheads of varying yields. The engine uses pre-packaged storable liquid propellants to generate 46,460lbs. of thrust over a six-second burn time, giving a maximum range of 75 miles with a nuclear payload. Lance is no longer in production, but additional nuclear warheads are being procured by the US Army, including those of the enhanced radiation type to be held in reserve in the United States.

The missile is normally deployed on a tracked launcher accompanied by a loader-transporter vehicle. Both vehicles are derived from the M548 and are jointly classified as the M667 Lance

Missile Carrier. The M667 is the basic chassis for the following applications in the Lance system: the M752 Launcher, Guided Missile, Carrier Mounted which transports one missile on the launcher, and the M688 Loader-Transporter, Guided Missile which carries two missiles and a crane to load the M572 Launcher.

The US Army has six Lance battalions with a total of 36 launchers deployed in Europe, with a further two battalions in CONUS. The Lance is also in service with the armies of Great Britain, Israel, Italy, West Germany, Belgium and Holland, although not all these countries have nuclear warheads.

M727 HAWK Self-Propelled Surface-to-Air Missile System

The principal low- and medium-altitude air-defence missile in the US field forces, HAWK (Homing-All-the-Way-Killer) has been in service since 1962. The basic HAWK system lacked mobility, so a self-propelled version was devised based on a derivative of the M548, designated M727. The prototype of the M727 was completed in 1966.

The M727 HAWK Missile Carrier is similar to the M730 used with the Chaparral SAM system. Each carrier mounts three missiles which face forward over the cab during transit. In the firing mode, the missiles point rearwards for launching. A blast deflector, which can be lifted hydraulically for engine maintenance, protects the cab during missile launch. A suspension lock-out provides a rigid platform for firing, and electrical power for the missile system is produced by a generator driven by a power take-off from the vehicle engine.

The solid-propellant missile carries a proximity-fused HE warhead of 165lbs., weighs 1,400lbs. and is $16\frac{1}{2}$ft. long. The guidance system is based

There have been numerous designs to develop a fire support vehicle based on the M113, to provide greater firepower in mechanised units without incurring the high costs of an MBT. One of the first and one of the few to see active service is the M113A1 FSV (Saladin) of the Australian Army. Sixteen of these vehicles were produced by marrying the 76mm-armed turret of the Saladin armoured car with an M113A1. It has now been superseded by a similar vehicle mounting a Scorpion CVR(T) turret. FMC offer an M113 FSV armed with a 90mm Cockerill gun in a Cadillac Gage turret, while Israeli Military Industries have produced a remarkable version known as MSWS Medium Support Weapon System armed with a hyper-velocity 60mm gun capable of armour penetrations greater than the British L7 105mm gun used in so many Western MBTs. (Department of Defence, Canberra)

The majority of M113 users employ an armoured ambulance version for the evacuation of battle casualties, capable of carrying four stretcher cases or walking wounded. Every M113 APC has standard fittings for conversion to this role. Displaying red crosses, this M113A1 APC(A) [Ambulance] of the Australian Army is pointedly named BLOOD BATH. (Department of Defence, Canberra)

on the semi-active principle.

A self-propelled HAWK platoon consists of three M727s, each carrying three missiles and towing one piece of ground equipment of the tracking and acquisition radars. Improved HAWK, first deployed in 1972, is capable of engaging aircraft from less than 100ft. to more than 38,000ft. in all weathers. The maximum effective range is about 25 miles. Self-propelled HAWK has only seen service with the US Army and Israel.

XM806E1 Recovery Vehicle: Full Tracked, Light Armored

An armoured recovery vehicle XM806 based on the M113 was developed under Project ENSURE during the Vietnam War for ARVN cavalry regiments operating in the Mekong Delta.

The XM806 was petrol driven, while the XM806E1 is an adaptation of the M113A1. It is equipped with a hydraulically driven winch inside the hull for retrieving immobilised vehicles under combat conditions. Winching operations may be accomplished with the ramp down and a protective guard in place, or through the ramp door, which gives additional protection for the operator. A spade is mounted on either side of the rear hull for use as a ground anchor when winching. An additional spade unit, stowed on the hull roof, may be mounted between the two outer ones for

recovery in soft conditions. A manually operated hydraulic crane can be mounted on the left side of the hull for battlefield replacement of major components. A crew of three operate the XM806E1 and its equipment. The vehicle has not been type-classified by the US Army, hence the experimental designation. In the Australian Army it is known as the M806A1 Armoured Recovery Vehicle (Light).

M901 Anti-Tank Combat Vehicle (Improved TOW Vehicle) (ITV)

The M901 is an M113A1 or M113A2 APC fitted with an elevating two-launcher TOW turret which allows the missiles to be fired from hull defilade or from behind buildings with only the head of the launcher exposed to hostile view.

Developed by Emerson Electric Company, the first production vehicles were deployed to Europe in early 1980. The US Army has a requirement for 1,952 M901s to replace the older M113 TOW carriers in mechanised infantry battalions. The M901 is also employed by some armoured cavalry units (see Plate F2), pending introduction of the M3 Cavalry Fighting Vehicle. A five-man crew is prescribed for this role, with the extra man acting as an observer. In cavalry units the vehicle is not known as ITV but CTV, standing for Cavalry TOW Vehicle.

The launcher pod is raised and lowered by lifting arms and incorporates standard TOW day and night sights as well as a three-power target acquisition sight that can detect hostile AFVs at several thousand yards. The sight is set at $13\times$ for missile aiming and guidance. The sight picture is relayed to the gunner located in the vehicle hull by means of an image-transfer assembly. The turret has $360°$ traverse at $35°$ per second, and an elevation range from $+34°$ to $-30°$.

From the moment the vehicle halts, it takes only 20 seconds for the launcher to be raised and for the target to be engaged. A second missile can be fired within five seconds of first-round impact. The launcher is then tilted back to be reloaded through the partly open rear cargo hatch by a crewman who is protected from small arms fire by armoured side flaps and overhead cover. Reloading the two missiles can be accomplished in less than 40 seconds. In addition to the two missiles in the launcher, ten TOWs are carried inside the vehicle. The TOW equipment can be removed from the vehicle and set up on a standard ground mount in less than one minute, if required. When travelling, the launcher is rotated through 180° and lowered on to the top of the hull to reduce height and obscure its distinctive profile. The M901 has a crew of four and weighs 13 tons combat loaded.

XM981 Fire Support Team Vehicle (FIST)

The XM981 is a forward observer's vehicle that will enter service with the US Army in the near future. Originally designated FOV for Forward Observer's Vehicle, the name has been changed to Fire Support Team Vehicle to avoid confusion with the acronym FOV, which applies to the M113 'Family of Vehicles' embracing the complete range of the M113 series. Based on the M113A2 APC, the XM981 is equipped for use by artillery forward observers in mechanised and armoured units. It is being developed by Emerson Electric Company and looks almost identical to the M901 ITV.

FIST uses a modified version of the TOW armoured launcher assembly, housing observation devices and a laser rangefinder locator-designator

combination to illuminate targets for the Copperhead 155mm M712 Cannon-Launched Guided Projectile or other Precision Guided Munitions. The turret raises, lowers and rotates in the same manner as on the M901, and the only slight difference in appearance is the size and shape of the central opening in the pod face.

FIST is equipped with extensive communications equipment and a satellite-based position-locating system to fix positions with extreme accuracy. A digital message-entry device is being developed to eliminate the need for voice communications with artillery command posts and firing units. Also under development is a 50ft. telescopic extension incorporating at the mast-head thermal-imaging, forward-looking infra-red (FLIR) sights, as well as daylight optics featuring low-light-level television. This facility will improve line-of-sight observation while allowing the vehicle to stay under cover and will double the area in view as compared to ground-level observation. Using the mast and daylight optics, targets can be

With missiles ready to fire on the M54 launch station, an M730 Chaparral Missile Carrier acts in the air defence role. The derivation of the M730 from the M548 Cargo Carrier is readily apparent. The aluminium hoops stowed at the front are ribs for a tarpaulin covering the rear bed and missile launcher in the travelling mode. (FMC Corporation)

HAWK missiles are elevated into firing position over the rear of an M727 HAWK Missile Carrier. Self-propelled HAWK did not prove as successful as the towed version and it has been phased out of service. (FMC Corporation)

laser-designated at five kilometres, while the night sight is effective to about two and a half kilometres, as well as being useful in bad weather or battlefield smoke.

AIFV—Armored Infantry Fighting Vehicle

In 1967, FMC was awarded a contract by the US Army to build two experimental carriers based on M113 components under the designation XM765, to fulfil the Army's requirement for a Mechanized Infantry Combat Vehicle incorporating a fully enclosed weapon system and firing ports for the infantry squad. Despite successful trials, the US Army did not adopt the XM765, but FMC continued to develop the design as a private venture, resulting in a new vehicle known as Product Improved M113A1 which appeared in 1970.

After extensive testing and further development involving a new 25mm gun turret, and the re-location of the commander's station from behind the 20mm gun cupola (as fitted on the PI M113A1) to a position alongside the new turret, a prototype was built in 1977 of a model called AIFV (Armored Infantry Fighting Vehicle). Funding for this development was supported by the Dutch Army, which placed an order for 800 vehicles in 1975 and received the first production AIFV in 1977. Subsequently the Army of the Philippines purchased the AIFV, and in July 1979 514 AIFVs were ordered by the Belgian Army.

The AIFV features a one-man enclosed weapon station mounting a 25mm Oerlikon KBA cannon and co-axial machine gun with day/night passive sights. The 25mm cannon is capable of defeating all light armoured vehicles at normal battle ranges, while its HE projectiles are highly effective against ground and aerial targets; 180 ready rounds are linked to the gun with an additional 147 in reserve.

Ten men including the driver, gunner and commander are carried by the AIFV, with six infantrymen facing outwards from the centre benches and a seat for a man to sit between the commander and the turret basket. There are two vision blocks and two firing ports in either side of the rear compartment for observation and for suppressive fire to be delivered in appropriate circumstances. A similar facility is available to the rear.

The AIFV embodies a considerable advance on the M113 in armour protection through the use of spaced laminate armour over critical areas of the welded aluminium hull and turret, while the upper hull sides and the hull front are sloped for superior ballistic protection. For increased safety, the crew are completely separated from the fuel tanks, which are mounted externally at the rear. Mobility is also improved over the M113 owing to the more powerful turbo-charged version of the Detroit Diesel 6V53 engine and the superior high strength torsion bar suspension.

As with the M113, a family of vehicles is based on the AIFV including a command post version, mortar prime mover, TOW missile vehicle, cargo carrier and ambulance.

Tracked Rapier

Proven in combat during the Falklands conflict, the Rapier low-level guided weapon system is being procured by the British Army in a new configuration mounted on a tracked vehicle to provide air defence against low-level attack for the battlegroups of BAOR.

Tracked Rapier is based on a version of the M548, classified as RCM748, with the main alteration being the addition of an armoured cab to the front of the vehicle. To the rear of the cab is a blast shield which protects the forward part of the vehicle when a missile is fired. The Rapier launcher is mounted on the rear bed of the RCM748 and is armour-protected, as are the four-round missile bins to either side. The command aerial is mounted on an elevating mechanism which allows missiles to be fired and

An M901 Improved TOW Vehicle fires a TOW anti-tank missile from its elevating launcher assembly. The vehicles illustrated are based on M113A2 APCs, incorporating M239 smoke grenade launchers of British design. Note the launcher assemblies of the two M901s in the background are lowered on to their hull tops. The M901 is called by troops 'Hammerhead' because of the resemblance of the TOW launcher to the shark of the same name. (Emerson Electric Company)

The XM981 Fire Support Team Vehicle (FISTV) is equipped with extensive and sophisticated communications and electronics, and laser designator equipment for use by artillery forward observers. It is almost identical in appearance to the M901 ITV but has external fuel tanks at the rear to save internal stowage space. FISTV enters production in 1983. In operation, FISTV acquires a target, with its own position established in earth co-ordinates, and 'lases' the target. The range, azimuth and elevation are automatically sent to the Digital Message Device to be communicated to the Battery Fire Direction Center. The artillery battery then opens fire, hitting the target with a minimal probability of error. (Emerson Electric Company)

guided at low elevations over the cab.

An optical tracker is mounted in the roof of the cab through which the operator tracks the target, steering the system with a joystick control and thereby establishing an optical sight line to the target. Collimated with this optical system is a TV tracker, which measures the displacement of the missile from the sight line so that correcting commands can be transmitted to the missile; this is first used to gather, and subsequently to control the missile to fly along the sight line until impact.

The Rapier missile is identical to that used in the towed system. The missile is manufactured as a round of ammunition and requires no maintenance, testing or servicing. It has a range of over 6,500 metres and is effective from ultra low level to over 3,000 metres. Once the eight missiles have been fired, Tracked Rapier can be reloaded in under five minutes without recourse to a crane. Twenty replenishment missiles together with personnel and messing equipment for the Fire Unit are carried in a standard M548 Support Vehicle.

In order to allow operations at night and in poor weather conditions a Blindfire radar can be added to the Fire Unit, either towed in its wheeled form or mounted in the rear of an RCM748 vehicle.

From a tactical move Tracked Rapier can be put into action and commence an engagement within 30 seconds of coming to a halt; the whole sequence is performed by the three-man crew from within the safety of the cab. Precise levelling of the vehicle and equipment is not necessary, and the crew only have to leave the cab to reload missiles. Fifty Tracked Rapier vehicles are on order for the British Army.

M113 Inventories

Argentina	140	— delivered 1967–69.
Australia	791	— includes 63 Fire Support Vehicles (15 FSV Saladin and 48 FSV Scorpion).
Belgium		— 525 M113A1 and 514 AIFV being built under licence in Belgium.
Bolivia	14	
Brazil	600	
Canada	800	
Chile	300	
Colombia	25	— delivered 1977.
Costa Rica		— small number in service.
Denmark	670	— includes 250 built by Oto Melara.
Ecuador	20	— delivered 1966.
Egypt	50	— delivered 1980. Approximately 850 of A2 series on order including M577A2, M548 and 38 M901.
El Salvador		— small number in service.
Ethiopia	28	— further deliveries embargoed.
Germany (FRG)	3,800	— all with diesel engines including 408 M106A1 with Tampella 120mm mortar, 100 M577A1,

IFAB artillery forward observer vehicles and radar carriers for RATAC and Green Archer.

Greece	700	— further quantities on order.
Guatemala	10	
Haiti	12	
Iran	600	
Iraq		— small quantity in use captured from Iran.
Israel	6,500	— numerous detail changes for various roles.
Italy	3,500	— most built under licence by Oto Melara. Includes VCC-1 Camillino, a modified version of M113A1 similar in configuration to FMC's Product Improved M113A1.
Jordan	933	— includes M113A1/A2 and M163. 8 M901 and 50 other units on order.
Kampuchea		serviceability doubtful.

Korea (ROK)	200	
Kuwait		— 6 M548 delivered, about 200 M113A2 family on order.
Laos		— serviceability doubtful.
Lebanon	97	— includes 28 delivered 1980 with further 210 on order including 69 M113A2, 27 M125A2 and 8 M577A2.
Libya	100	— built by Oto-Melara.
Morocco	548	— includes 59 M163.
Netherlands	800	— does not include AIFV.
New Zealand	66	
Norway	120	— some with Hägglunds turret and Rh202 Rheinmetall 20mm cannon, vehicle designated NM135.
Pakistan	750	— further 100 on order.
Peru	300	
Philippines	49	— also AIFV on order.
Portugal	111	— further 9 M125A2 and

Tracked Rapier is based on an armoured version of the M548 known as the RCM 748. Between the four-round missile bins is the surveillance radar and IFF radome with the command aerial (above) in the elevated position. On the armoured cab roof is the optical/TV tracking system and at the forward corners the low-profile radio antennae. (RSA)

Israeli M113A1 APCs land on the coast of Lebanon during Operation 'Peace for Galilee'. These vehicles show the standard configuration of Israeli APCs, with a .50cal. M2HB at the commander's cupola and two FN 7.62mm MAG machine guns either side of the troop compartment. A Soltam 60mm Commando mortar is also fitted to the roof of Israeli M113 APCs to provide coverage over ranges from 100-800 metres. (IDF)

		18 M113A2/TOW on order.
Saudi Arabia	900	— further units on order.
Singapore	520	— further 185 M113A2 and 22 XM806E1 on order.
Somalia		— small number in service.
Spain	750	
Sudan		— 66 on order.
Switzerland	1,475	— M113 designated Schutzenpanzer 63, 500 APCs armed with 20mm gun turret of

		Swedish Pbv 302 APC, designated SPz 63/73. Further 160 M548 on order.
Taiwan	248	
Thailand	400	— 24 M163 on order.
Tunisia	96	— further 65 on order.
Turkey	2,000	— 129 purchased, 1,871 donated under MAP.
United Kingdom		— Lance and Tracked Rapier.
USA	24,000	— Approximately half are squad carriers.
Vietnam		— number unknown.
Uruguay	15	
Yemen (UAR)	50	— paid for by Saudi Arabia.
Zaire	54	

Note: many of the vehicles on order in the above list will have been delivered by now.

The Plates

A1: M113 APC of 21st Mechanised Rifle Company, ARVN 21st Division; Mekong Delta, 1962

In the first months of operations in the Mekong Delta some ARVN M113 APCs were painted in this camouflage scheme. However, such schemes were short-lived and were never officially endorsed. Henceforth, with few exceptions, ARVN APCs were painted standard US Army Olive Drab, because it was deemed impossible to conceal an AFV which was either in motion or firing—in the words of the Senior American Armor Advisor to the ARVN Armor Command, 'Fifty tons of camouflage-painted pig iron looks like fifty tons of camouflage-painted pig iron.' This colour scheme was devised to enhance the psychological shock effect of the APCs, which at this time were dubbed 'Green Dragons'.

The insignia depict: (1) The shoulder patch of ARVN armour personnel, with the device in the circle at the upper left indicating the formation—the lightning bolt (illustrated) indicates Head-quarters Armor Command. The Armor School had a three-flamed 'lamp of knowledge'. The regiments, both Cavalry and Tank, used the appropriate Arabic numerals, while the four armoured brigades used Roman numerals. (2) The branch insignia, either in metal or cloth (illustrated), was worn over the right breast pocket. US advisers were awarded this badge upon their counterpart's recommendation, and wear it to this day as a 'Combat Armor Badge'. (3) ARVN armour personnel wore a distinguishing black beret (worn pulled to the right, as opposed to all other arms which wore theirs to the left) adorned with a badge by which the basic grade level of the wearer could be determined. Enlisted men wore a simple silver tank; NCOs wore the tank enclosed in a silver circle; company grade officers had a gold circle (illustrated); and field grade officers wore a tank enclosed by a gold wreath. General officers wore the appropriate number of stars between the tips of the wreath.

A2: M113 APC of the Armor Regiment, ROK Capital Division; Qui Nhon, II Corps Tactical Zone, South Vietnam 1967

Reminiscent of the gaudy colour schemes adopted during the Korean War (cf. Vanguard 27 *Armour of the Korean War*), South Korean M113 APCs of the Republic of Korea Capital Division were painted in tiger stripes with a tiger's head on the

Vehicles from the Forward Company of an Ordnance battalion follow advancing IDF armour during Operation 'Peace for Galilee' in the Lebanon, June 1982. Experiences in the October War of 1973 revealed the vital necessity of rapid repair and recovery for armoured units in order to maintain offensive capabilities. Accordingly, forward elements of Israeli Ordnance Corps personnel are now fully mobile, employing a variety of specialized vehicles including the venerable M3 half-track and the M113A1 Fitter's Vehicle—seen below the Super Frelon beyond the M113A1 Armoured Ambulance, marked with red Stars of David, of a medical unit. (IDF)

Légionnaires of the French Foreign Legion's 2ᵉ REP watch warily as Israeli troops evacuate the port area of Beirut, September 1982. The rear doors of Israeli APCs are painted white as a mutual recognition device. (Légion Etrangère)

trim vane, reflecting the formation's sobriquet — 'the Tigers'. The inscription on the hull front is Korean for 'tiger'.

B1: M113A1 APC of the Reconnaissance Platoon, Headquarters and Headquarters Company, 4th Battalion, 23rd Infantry (Mechanized) of 25th Infantry Division: Trang Bang, South Vietnam, 1968
Mounting ACAV hatch armour and gunshield for the .50cal. Browning, this M113A1 APC of 4/23rd (Mech) is adorned with a pig's head and is named THE UGLY AMERICAN, after the book by William Lederer and Eugene Burdick which was highly critical of America's involvement in South-East Asia. All vehicle markings are painted in white but are tainted with red dust, characteristic of the rubber-growing areas of Vietnam.

B2: M577A1 Armored Command Post of Headquarters and Headquarters Troop, 1st Squadron, 4th Cavalry of 1st Infantry Division; III Corps Tactical Zone, South Vietnam, 1968
US AFVs rarely carried camouflage schemes during the Vietnam War, as they served little purpose in the circumstances and against the enemy encountered. This M577A1 of the 'Quarter-horse' sports dark green stripes over the Olive Drab base colour, as well as a drawing on the hull side

of the cartoon character 'Road Runner', after whom was named one of the standard missions conducted by armour units in Vietnam. On the roof of the M577A1 are two armoured helicopter pilot's seats salvaged from damaged 'choppers'.

C1: M106A1 4.2in. Mortar Carrier of Troop I, 3rd Squadron, 11th Armored Cavalry Regiment; III Corps Tactical Zone, South Vietnam, 1969
In Vietnam the Support Squads of Armored Cavalry Platoons in both divisional and regimental Armored Cavalry Squadrons were equipped with the M106 4.2in. Mortar Carrier. However, as the minimum effective range of the M30 mortar was greater than the distance of the majority of fire-fights, and it was therefore unable to bring fire to bear in many contacts, M106s were commonly grouped at troop or squadron level to give area coverage. This 'four-deuce' tows a 1½-ton M332 ammunition trailer carrying additional mortar rounds for extended firing. The bumper numbers '11ACR' 'I-29' denote 2nd Armored Cavalry Platoon of Troop I, 3rd Squadron, 11th Armored Cavalry Regiment, while '9' was the number of the support squad vehicle. The detail view shows the stencilled inscription on the commander's cupola hatch, which adorned many AFVs of the 'Blackhorse Regiment'. Its sentiments are self-evident.

C2: M548 Cargo Carrier of 168th Engineer Battalion, 79th Engineer Group; III Corps Tactical Zone, South Vietnam, 1969
The M548 Cargo Carrier was widely used in Vietnam to support armoured and mechanised units across forbidding terrain that defied the passage of wheeled supply vehicles. MOTHER TRUCKER served with a Land Clearing Company of 168th Engineer Battalion, 79th Engineer Group of 20th Engineer Brigade within II Field Force in III CTZ.

D1: M113A1 APC of 3 Troop, B Squadron, 3rd Cavalry Regiment, RAAC; Phuoc Tuy Province, South Vietnam, 1970
Australian APCs in Vietnam were progressively fitted with machine gun cupolas during the war to provide greater protection to vehicle commanders, the type illustrated being the Cadillac-Gage T-50

on an M113A1 APC. The vehicle callsign '31A' was displayed on the rear ramp and on the vehicle sides on detachable metal plates, with '31' and 'Alpha' either side of the B Squadron sign of a red square: '31A' denotes the second vehicle of 1st Section, 3 Troop. The insignia of IATF and the registration number '134288' is borne on the rear bumpers. The vehicle is named & TEARS after the rock group Blood, Sweat and Tears; the other two vehicles of 1st Section being BLOOD and SWEAT. Other sections named their APCs in a similar manner, such as THE GOOD, THE BAD and THE UGLY after the Clint Eastwood 'Spaghetti Western' film. Vehicle names ranged from the humorous to the bizarre, e.g. CAR FIFTY FOUR after the TV comedy series 'Car 54 Where Are You?' reflecting the problems of navigation in jungle terrain; rather less subtle is GOOKCRUSHER. Many vehicles sported maps of Australia with the state from which crew members originated painted in a different colour. Another common marking on the APCs of 3rd Cavalry was a scorpion. This was an unofficial insignia adopted by the cavalry on account of the prowess of the unit's pet scorpion in defeating all comers in duels to the death. The detail view shows the unofficial, locally-fabricated shoulder patch of 3 Troop.

D2: M113A1(FS) Fire Support Vehicle of the Support Troop, A Squadron, 3rd Cavalry Regiment; FSB Horseshoe, Phuoc Tuy Province, South Vietnam, 1971

Six M113A1(FS) Fire Support Vehicles served in Vietnam from early 1971 until the departure of 3rd Cavalry in March 1972. Two served in a Cavalry Troop and the others in two sections in a Support Troop. Finished in Australian Olive Green, THE BEAST carries its registration number '134712' front and rear. The callsign number '42A' is painted on both hull sides within the blue triangle of A Squadron, and is repeated on the rear door together with the insignia of 1st Australian Task Force—a red leaping kangaroo on a yellow shield. The yellow Xs on the barrel are a reminder of that excellent Queensland beer '4X'. The FSVs undertook many tasks, but were mainly employed for indirect fire from Fire Support Bases and for protection of Land Clearing Teams.

E: ACAVs in Vietnam

The majority of AFVs during the Vietnam War were innocent of graffiti, and even official markings were either obliterated or subdued; for reasons of survival, most crews did not wish to draw attention to their particular vehicle—conspicuous markings formed convenient aiming points for enemy RPGs. Some crews, however, were less prudent, and their vehicles displayed a gamut of extravagant designs.

E1: ACAV of Troop B, 3rd Squadron, 4th Cavalry, 1969

EL TORRO ('The Bull') carries on the gunshield a stylised regimental insignia with the squadron number above and with the vehicle callsign number to its side—'24', indicating the fourth vehicle of 2nd Platoon and the second vehicle of the second Scout Section. The sequence was: '20'—ACAV of platoon leader; '21' and '22'—ACAVs of first Scout Section; '23' and '24'—

Flying national flags, M113A2 ACAVs of the Lebanese Army move into West Beirut to relieve the French peace-keeping force, September 1982. (Légion Etrangère)

One of several new variants derived from the M113 currently entering service with the US Army is the Surface Launched Unit, Fuel Air Explosive (SLUFAE) Mine Neutralization System, which fires unguided rockets to disrupt enemy minefields by blast overpressure. (US Army)

ACAVs of second Scout Section; '25', '26' and '27'—Sheridans; '28'—infantry squad APC; and '29'—M106A1 'mortar track' of the Support Squad. The white triangle at hull rear is a troop colour code whereby the troop commander could identify his units at a glance: Troop A, red; Troop B, white; and Troop C, blue. The push-buttons of his radio were similarly colour-coded.

E2: ACAV of Troop E, 2nd Squadron, 11th Armored Cavalry Regiment, 1969
Prominently exhibited on the hull sides of this ACAV are the crossed sabres, symbol of the Cavalry Branch, and often painted on the AFVs and helicopters of cavalry units. The numbers '2' and '11' above and below the sabres denote 2nd Squadron, 11th Armored Cavalry Regiment. Above is the name CLOUD 9 as well as CATHY GIRL, a crewman's reminder of his girlfriend 'back in the World'. On the gunshield is EVIL 26, indicating the sixth vehicle of 2nd Armored Cavalry Platoon of Troop E, who adopted the callsign 'Evil' in preference to the official phonetic alphabet word 'Echo'; Troop K ('Kilo') called themselves 'Killer' Troop.

E3: ACAV of Troop A, 1st Squadron, 10th Cavalry, 1971
On the hullside WHY ME sports the cartoon character Snoopy firing a .50cal. Browning, and a

red-over-white cavalry guidon abaft the vehicle number. In 1/10th Cav the vehicle callsign numbers were colour-coded red, white and blue to indicate A, B and C Troops. WHY ME carries a plethora of names on its gunshields and hatch armour, OMERTÀ being the Mafia code of silence.

F1: M113A1 Carrier (Cavalry Scout Version) of 2nd Armored Cavalry Platoon, Troop B, 1st Squadron, 11th Armored Cavalry Regiment; Outpost Alpha, Fulda Gap, Germany, 1981
US Army Cavalry units are currently equipped with the M113 pending the introduction of the M3 Cavalry Fighting Vehicle. The M113A1 Cavalry Scout Version differs from the basic APC only in the combat loading. It has a crew of five—driver, commander/gunner, two observers with M203 'over and unders', and the fifth member manning the squad M60 MG. The Armored Cavalry Platoon comprises ten vehicles—'B-20' M113A1 (CSV) of the platoon commander; 'B-21' to 'B-24', M60A3 tanks; 'B-25' and 'B-26', M113A1 (CSV) with Dragon; 'B-27' and 'B-28', M901 Cavalry TOW Vehicles; 'B-29', M106A1 Mortar Carrier.

BULL RIDER is painted in the MERDC camouflage but the colours do not conform to an official scheme—not unusual in 7th Army. The vehicle mounts an FGM-77 Dragon ATGW (M175) beside the M2HB Browning to augment firepower and tank-killing capability; in this guise the vehicle is nicknamed 'Dragon Wagon' or 'Dragon Track'. The shield to the front of the weapon is simply a brush guard and provides no armour protection. The device on the hull front is a CBR detector. The bumper numbers are in subdued flat black, with from left to right: a Roman numeral 'V' denoting 5th Corps; 'I/II CAV', 1st Squadron, 11th Armored Cavalry Regiment; and 'B-25', the fifth vehicle of 2nd Platoon, Troop B.

F2: M577A1 Command Post Vehicle of Battery Battalion, Artillery, West Germany, 1978
In 1973 the US Army introduced a series of four-colour camouflage schemes devised by the Mobility Equipment Research and Development Command (MERDC) at Ford Belvoir, Virginia. During the acceptance trials, US 7th Army in

Europe created temporary patterns pending introduction of the formal MERDC schemes. While the latter uses two principal and two secondary colours, the 7th Army has three and one—Sand, Earth Red, Olive Drab and Black—as on this M577A1 named BUZZARD BRAINS. Although officially superseded by MERDC, many vehicles in Germany still retain these 'temporary' schemes.

G1: M113A2 APC of 8th Infantry Regiment, Royal Moroccan Army; Operation 'Ohoud', Western Sahara, 1979

The M113 is in service with over 50 armies around the world and has seen combat in virtually every conflict since the early 1960s. Operation 'Ohoud' was a large-scale offensive conducted by a force comprising 1,500 vehicles and 6,000 men of the Moroccan Army against the Polisario guerilla movement in the Sahara desert. Moroccan AFVs include French VAB APCs, Soviet 'Stalin Organ' rocket launchers (purchased from Rumania), Austrian Kürassier K tank destroyers (known as Iska in Moroccan service), and American M163 Vulcan air defence vehicles and M113A1/A2 APCs. The vehicles are painted overall desert sand, and the M113s feature the vehicle numbers in Arabic script prominently along the hull sides. The two white stripes on the trim vane are a recognition sign carried by all vehicles.

G2: M113A1 'Zelda' of the Israeli Defence Forces; Operation 'Peace for Galilee', Lebanon, 1982

The Israeli Defence Forces are the largest user of the M113 after the US Army, with over 6,000 in service. It is known as 'Zelda', which is a girl's name in Hebrew. The Zelda was extensively employed in numerous roles during Operation 'Peace for Galilee'. Israeli doctrine does not require that infantry fight mounted from APCs and, for the moment, sees no need for expensive mechanised infantry combat vehicles. The M113 is therefore

South Korean M113 APCs support a paratroop drop during manoeuvres near the Demilitarized Zone along the 38th Parallel. The vehicles are finished in the US MERDC temperate zone camouflage scheme. (ROK Army)

admirably suited to their concept of a combined-arms formation in which the APC transports infantry to the start-line for dismounted assault which tanks, the main component of armoured formations, cannot perform. The Israelis have made a number of detail changes to their M113 family of vehicles, such as the extension of the exhaust pipe down the hull side. The most significant operationally is the installation of external fuel tanks at the rear (as on the vehicle illustrated), both on new order vehicles and as a retrofit programme. During the October War the location of the fuel tank on the inside rear left-hand hull wall proved vulnerable on occasions, leading to catastrophic internal fires. The vehicle illustrated is finished in the sand grey colour characteristic of vehicles on the Northern Front.

The significance of the markings remains a matter of conjecture and unit identification is not known. The cerise panel is an air recognition sign.

H: M113A1 Interior, and Combat Loading Plan of M113A1 (Cavalry Scout Version)

This plate illustrates the interior of a typical M113A1 APC. The inside is painted Sea Foam Green because this colour is supposed to be psychologically the most restful in confined spaces. Besides the clutter of crew kitbags, ammunition boxes, combat rations, Dragon rocket launcher and other paraphernalia, two essential items carried by all APCs on operations are a beer cooler, and a map of the local area attached to the fuel tank.

Notes sur les planches en couleur

A1 Ancienne combinaison de peinture de camouflage, bientôt remplacée par du vert olive ordinaire. Les détails de l'insigne sont: (1) écusson de ARVN Armour Command HQ (2) insigne pectoral de droite des tankistes (3) badge d'officier subalterne, unités blindées ARVN, porté sur béret noir. **A2** Ce thème qui rappelle le camouflage criard utilisé au cours de la guerre de Corée compte l'insigne relatif au surnom de la division: 'Les tigres'.

B1 Le nom fait écho au titre du célèbre ouvrage qui critiqua le rôle des Etats-Unis dans le Sud-est asiatique: 'The Ugly American' (l'affreux américain). **B2** Les véhicules militaires américains étaient rarement camouflés mais celui-ci arbore des raies vertes. Remarquez le personnage de dessin animé 'Road Runner' et les sièges blindés fixés au toit du pilote d'hélicoptère 'libéré'.

C1 Les inscriptions indiquent le 11ème régiment de cavalerie blindée; neuvième véhicule, troupe I, section 2. Notez la remorque à munitions M332 avec ses projectiles de mortier supplémentaires. **C2** Le véhicule de charge M548 a été utilisé intensivement au Vietnam pour appuyer des unités mécanisées sur des terrains défiant le passage des véhicules à roues.

D1 Les véhicules blindés australiens étaient équipés de diverses tourelles: voici le Cadillac-Gage T50. '31A' est la désignation du deuxième véhicule, 1ère section, 3ème troupe et le carré rouge identifie l'escadron B. L'insigne au kangourou de la '1st Australian Task Force' est exhibé avec d'autres emblèmes officiels. Ce nom rappelle que les trois véhicules de cette section ont été baptisés d'après un groupe de rock: 'Blood', 'Sweat', 'and Tears'. **D2** Six véhicules équipés de la tourelle du blindé Saladin ont servi au Vietnam. Le triangle bleu identifie l'escadron A; et le kangourou rouge, 1ATF.

E1 Sabres de cavalerie dont le symbole '2' correspond à l'escadron 2, '11' = 11ACR. Plusieurs noms différents ont été peints par l'équipage, y compris l'indicatif semi-officiel 'Evil 26'—'E' pour 'Troupe E'. **E2** Insigne stylisé du régiment ainsi que le numéro de l'escadron '3' et l'indicatif du véhicule '24' peint sur le bouclier du canon d'un véhicule baptisé 'The Bull' (le taureau). Le triangle à l'arrière de la coque identifie la troupe: 'Troupe A', rouge; 'Troupe B', blanc; 'Troupe C', bleu. **E3** De nombreux noms et slogans couvrent un véhicule décoré du personnage de bandes dessinées 'Snoopy'. Dans cette unité, la séquence de couleur a été appliquée aux numéros d'indicatifs du véhicule.

F1 Malgré l'introduction à cette époque du camouflage officiel quadricolore pour l'armée américaine, de nombreuses unités en Allemagne continuaient à utiliser leur propre version non-officielle dont certaines persistent encore à l'heure actuelle. **F2** Motif de camouflage officiel MERDC, mais les couleurs sont officieuses. Les inscriptions sont: 'V' (V Corps), 'I/II CAV' (1er escadron, 11ème régiment de cavalerie blindée), 'B-25' (Troupe B, 2ème section, cinquième véhicule).

G1 Numéro particulier de véhicule en caractères arabes sur les côtés de la coque; les raies blanches sont un signe de reconnaissance arboré par tous les véhicules pour cette opération. **G2** Les modifications apportées par les Israéliens sont notamment des réservoirs de carburant à l'extérieur de la coque arrière et le prolongement sur le tuyau d'échappement. L'importance de ces inscriptions n'est pas connue.

H Pour des raisons d'espace, il serait bon que les lecteurs se reportent aux légendes en langue anglaise.

Farbtafeln

A1 Frühe Tarnfarben, bald darauf durch einfaches Olivgrün ersetzt. Abzeichen: (1) Schulterabzeichen des ARVN Armour Command HQ; (2) rechtes Brustabzeichen des bewaffneten Personals; (3) Abzeichen der jüngeren Offiziere der bewaffneten ARVN-Einheiten, auf dem schwarzen Barrett getragen. **A2** In Erinnerung an die lebhaften Tarnfarben, die im Korea-Krieg benutzt wurden, deutet das Abzeichen auf den Spitznamen der Abteilung an—'Die Tiger'.

B1 Der Name erinnert an das berühmte Buch, das die Rolle der USA in Südostasien kritisch untersucht: 'Der hässliche Amerikaner'. **B2** US-Fahrzeuge waren selten getarnt, aber dieses hier trägt grüne Streifen. Man beachte die Zeichen-trickfilm-Figur 'Roadrunner' und die auf dem Dach befestigten 'geklauten' Hubschrauber-Pilotensitze.

C1 Die Markierungen verweisen auf das II. Gepanzerte Kavallerie-Regiment, Truppe I, 2. Zug, neuntes Fahrzeug. Man beachte den M332 Munitionsanhänger mit zusätzlichen Granaten. **C2** Das M548 Kargo-Fahrzeug wurde in Vietnam vielfach eingesetzt, um mechanisierte Einheiten in Gebieten zu unterstützen, wo Fahrzeuge mit Rädern nicht zu benutzen waren.

D1 Australische Fahrzeuge waren mit verschiedenen Geschütztürmen ausgestattet, hier ein Cadillac-Gage T50. '31A' steht für zweites Fahrzeug, 1. Abteilung, 3. Truppe, und das rote Viereck verweist auf Schwadron B. Neben dem Känguruh-Abzeichen der 1. Australian Task Force (1ATF) sind andere inoffizielle Embleme. Die Namen der drei Fahrzeuge wurden von der Rockgruppe 'Blood, Sweat, & Tears' übernommen. **D2** Sechs Fahrzeuge mit dem Geschützturm des Panzerwagens 'Saladin' wurden in Vietnam eingesetzt. Das blaue Dreieck steht für Schwadron A, das rote Känguruh für 1ATF.

E1 Kavallerie-Säbel; '2' = Schwadron 2, '11' = 11ACR. Verschiedene Namen wurden von den Soldaten aufgemalt, darunter das halboffizielle Rufzeichen 'Evil 26'—'E' steht für Truppe E. **E2** Stilisierte Regimentszeichen, zusammen mit der Schwadron-Nummer '3' und dem Fahrzeug-Rufzeichen '24' auf den Kugelschild eines Fahrzeugs mit dem Namen 'Der Bulle' gemalt. Das Dreieck an der Hinterseite der Karosserie verweist auf die Truppe—Truppe A: rot, Truppe B: weiss, Truppe C: blau. **E3** Viele Namen und Slogans auf einem mit einem 'Snoopy'-Bild dekorierten Fahrzeug. In dieser Einheit wurden die Farben für Fahrzeug-Rufzeichennummern benutzt.

F1 Während zu dieser Zeit die offizielle Vierfarben-Tarnung der US Armee eingeführt wurde, benutzten viele Einheiten in Deutschland ihre eigenen, inoffiziellen Versionen, von denen einige noch heute existieren. **F2** Offizielle MERDC-Tarnung mit inoffiziellen Farben. Markierungen: 'V' (Korps V), 'I/II CAV' (I. Schwadron, II. Gepanzertes Kavallerie-Regiment), 'B-25' (Truppe B, 2. Zug, fünftes Fahrzeug).

G1 Individuelle Fahrzeugnummer in arabischen Ziffern auf den Karosserieseiten; weisse Streifen sind das bei dieser Operation von allen Fahrzeugen getragene Erkennungszeichen. **G2** Israelische Änderungen waren u.a. das Anbringen der Benzintanks an der Aussenseite der hinteren Karosserie und eine Verlängerung des Auspuffs. Die Bedeutung der Markierungen ist unbekannt.

H Aus Platzgründen wird der Leser auf die englischen Bildunterschriften verwiesen.